SKILLS IN
FOOD
TECHNOLOGY

Jenny Ridgwell

Heinemann is an imprint of Pearson Education Limited, a company incorporated in England and Wales, having its registered office at Edinburgh Gate, Harlow, Essex, CM20 2JE. Registered company number: 872828

Heinemann is the registered trademark of Pearson Education Limited

First published 1997

2008
15 14 13 12 11 10

British Library Cataloguing in Publication Data

A catalogue record for this book is available from the British Library

ISBN 978 043 542082 6

Designed and typeset by Dennis Fairey & Associates Ltd

Illustrated by Arthur Phillips, Piers Sanford and Bill Lisle

Printed and bound in Scotland by Scotprint

Acknowledgements

The publishers would like to thank the following for permission to reproduce copyright material:

Asda for the label on p. 60; The British Nutrition Foundation for the extract on p. 4; Canland UK Ltd for the material on p. 67; Fletchers Bakeries for the reoriginated label on p. 41; Food MicroModel Ltd for the page from *Food MicroModel* on p. 69; Grisewood & Dempsey Ltd for an extract from *My First Encyclopedia –How Things Are Made*, by Steve Parker published by Kingfisher on pp. 8–9. Copyright Text © Grisewood & Dempsey Ltd 1994. Copyright Illustrations © Grisewood & Dempsey Ltd/Larousse Jeunesse 1992; The Guild of Food Writers for the leaflet on p. 43;

Hampshire Microtechnology Centre for the pizza label from *Nutrients* on pp. 38, 93; Health Education Authority for the illustration from *The Balance of Good Health* on p. 36; Heinz for the label on p. 85; HMSO for the extract from *Characteristics of Good Practice in Food Technology* on p. 4. Crown copyright is reproduced with the permission of the Controller of Her Majesty's Stationery Office; Institute of Food Science and Technology for the extracts on pp. 45, 55; Marks & Spencer plc for the label on p. 21, the Healthier Choice symbols on p. 37, the photo on p. 39 and the label on p. 53; Linda McCartney for the vegetarian symbol on p. 96; McVities UK for the diagram on p. 75; Meat and Livestock Commission for the recipe on p. 61; Ministry of Agriculture, Fisheries and Food for the tables on pp. 37, 38 from *Use your label: making sense of nutrition information* (PB2362) © Crown copyright; The National Dairy Council for the tables on pp. 12–13; The New Covent Garden Soup Company Ltd for the label on p. 60, the label on p. 71, the range of soups on p. 80, the adapted recipe and the carton on p. 81, the carton on p. 82 and the extract on p. 83; Pizza Hut (UK) Ltd for the packaging on p. 72; Pret à Manger for the Mission Statement on p. 55; The Royal Society of Chemistry for the nutritional analysis figures from *Composition of Foods* by McCance and Widdowson on p. 39; J Sainsbury plc for the Healthy Eating symbol on p. 36, the Cheese Strength Guide on p. 59, the reoriginated label on p. 60, the label on p. 63, the ingredients chart on p. 77 and the label on p. 78; Solo/Daily Mail for the article from the *Daily Mail*, 22/1/96 on p. 79; Tandoori Magazine for the article from *Tandoori Magazine*, March 1997 on p. 25; The Telegraph Group Ltd for the article on p. 18 'Mrs Beeton not to blame for food poisoning' by Paul Stokes, published 24/9/94 in The *Daily Telegraph* © Telegraph Group Limited, London, 1994; Tesco Stores Ltd for the label on p. 14 and the Healthy Eating symbol on p. 36; The Vegetarian Society for the symbols on p. 76; (Chocolate Chip Muffins) Based on Easy Breakfast Muffins taken from *The Walker Children's Fun-to-Cook Book* on p. 40 Text © 1996 Roz Denny and Caroline Waldegrave. Reproduced by permission of the publisher Walker Books Ltd.

The publishers would like to thank the following for permission to use photographs:

Ace photos p. 93; Canland UK Ltd p. 67; Kenwood Ltd p. 26; Leatherhead Food RA pp. 69, 93; McCain (GB) Ltd p. 64; J. Sainsbury plc p. 56; Sanyo UK Ltd p. 27; Roger Scruton pp. 13, 27 (probes supplied by ETI Ltd), 28, 29, 34, 38, 47 (probes supplied by ETI Ltd), 53, 59, 68, 78, 88; Shahi Tandoor p. 25; SIS p. 67.

The publishers would like to thank Aricot Vert Designs for permission to reproduce the cover photograph.

The publishers have made every effort to trace copyright holders. However, if any material has been incorrectly acknowledged, we would be pleased to correct this at the earliest opportunity.

Contents

What is food technology?

The aim of studying **food technology** is to develop your skills and knowledge to design and make good quality food products. The British Nutrition Foundation defines food technology as:

the process involved in the conversion of **raw materials** to edible food products including meals.

The DfEE publication *Characteristics of Good Practice in Food Technology* states:

food technology helps pupils to understand the physical, chemical, nutritional, biological and **sensory properties of foods** and how to exploit these properties when designing and making food products.

What knowledge and skills do you need to learn?

The areas you will cover when studying food technology include:

- analysing and following a design brief
- learning about food ingredients and their uses in food products
- nutrition and nutritional analysis
- food science
- understanding the process of food product development
- hygiene and safety
- quality and how it can be measured
- sensory testing
- writing a specification and testing against it
- learning about industrial food production on a large scale
- developing skills in food preparation and cooking
- evaluating and testing food products
- learning about food packaging and labelling
- using **information technology (IT)** to support product design.

The activities in this book can be used for focused practical tasks (FPTs) and activities in which you investigate, **disassemble** and evaluate (IDEAs) as well as design and make activities (DMAs) which are all part of the National Curriculum design and technology.

The spider charts below show the range of knowledge and skills linked to food product development.

HACCP stands for Hazard Analysis and Critical Control Point – see pages 50–51.

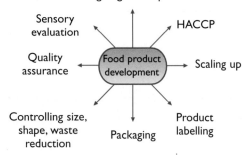

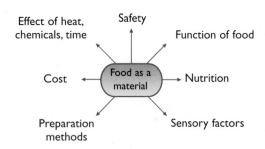

Spider charts on food product development, food as a material and recipe development

4

The food industry

What knowledge and skills does industry need to design and make food products?

Steps in product development

1 Design teams work on product design.

2 Food scientists investigate food products and apply food science to product development.

3 Food buyers look for the best ingredients.

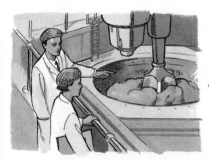

6 Technologists design equipment for large-scale production.

5 All food workers know about hygiene and safety.

4 Experts taste and test foods.

7 Nutritionists help with food analysis.

8 Experts design packaging and labelling.

Questions

1 What do you think is meant by 'food technology'?

2 What are the roles of the following people in food product design?

a food scientist
b food buyer
c nutritionists

Some of the skills and knowledge needed to carry out a food technology activity

Food handling skills	Examples
measuring and weighing accurately	using digital scales for accurate measurement, designing precise recipes **(formulations)** which can be made in quantity
food handling skills	peeling, chopping, slicing, grating, mashing and mixing foods; rolling, folding and shaping foods
using a range of tools and equipment accurately and safely	learning how to use sharp knives and food processors
assembling food	being able to put together a range of food products such as soups, cakes, biscuits, stir fries, curries, dips and salads
energy use	being able to use different methods of cooking
hygiene	knowing how to work safely and hygienically and keep food at the right temperature
sensory evaluation	carrying out accurate and fair tasting sessions to help with design ideas
planning	being able to write and follow plans

Some essential food handling skills that are needed for food preparation

Making one food into another

Food technology is about changing raw materials into good quality food products. It starts with the raw materials – the first stage of a food before it is made into something else. Raw materials include eggs, apples, potatoes, fish and grains of wheat.

Some of these foods can be eaten raw (for example, apples) but others have to be changed into food products. This stage is called **primary processing**. Wheat grains are changed into flour and then made into edible products such as bread, cakes and biscuits. Milk is pasteurized to make it safer to use, then it can be made into cheese, yogurt and ice-cream. This stage is known as **secondary processing**.

Wheat (raw material)
Primary processing: cleaned and ground into flour
Secondary processing: made into pastry for a pie

Orange (raw material)
Primary processing: squeezed into orange juice
Secondary processing: made into ice lolly

Stages in the processing of wheat and oranges into food products

Questions

1 List *ten* foods that can be eaten raw, without further processing.

2 Describe how *three* raw foods can be used to make other products – for example, apples are made into apple juice.

3 List as many food products as you can that are made from:

a different types of flour
b milk.

Compare your results with those of others.

How food products are made

Most of the food that we eat is made on a large scale in factories, bakeries and food-processing plants. Here are some examples of how everyday food products are made.

Roasted peanuts

1 The peanuts are shaken on a grid: the shells break apart and the nuts fall out.

2 Sorting machines check and remove bits of shell and grit.

3 Peanuts are blanched by putting them in hot water to split the red skins. Metal rollers shake the peanuts to remove the skins.

4 Peanuts are roasted in hot oil for five minutes.

5 Roasted nuts are weighed and wrapped by a bagging machine.

Some nuts are sent to other factories to make peanut butter.

Fizzy orange drink

1 Oranges are squeezed into juice which is sold to the fizzy drink manufacturers.

2 At the drinks factory, ingredients such as water and sugar (or artificial sweetener) are added to the juice and carbon dioxide gas is forced into the mixture to make the drink fizzy.

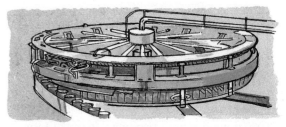

3 The drink is squirted into cans and a machine called a seamer puts the lids on the cans.

Bread in a bakery

In a large bakery, the mixing, baking, cooling and slicing processes are controlled by computers.

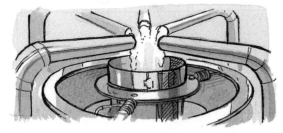

1 The ingredients are weighed and poured into a high-speed mixer, and mixed into a soft dough.

2 The dough is cut into loaves and the loaves are put on trays to prove and increase in size.

3 The bread is baked in a hot oven, then cooled.

4 Some bread is sliced, and the bread is wrapped by machine ready for distribution.

Drawing a flow diagram

A flow diagram is a series of steps to show the process of making a product. You can draw these steps in boxes, or as a list of steps – for example, 'Step 1 Measure ingredients'. See pages 48–49 for more information.

Fish fingers

1 Fish arrives in the factory, and the filleting machine cuts the flesh from the bones.

2 The fish is frozen into large blocks.

3 The blocks are sliced, coated with breadcrumbs and cooked in hot oil.

4 Frozen fish fingers are packed into boxes ready for distribution.

Taken from an original concept by Young World, How Things are Made, *Kingfisher Books*

Question

Draw flow diagrams to show the process for making *two* of the food products shown on these pages. What checks would need to be made at each stage to make sure the product was safe to eat and of good quality?

Designing a food product

These are some of the stages you may go through when designing and making a food product.

analyse the design brief
⬇
gather research information
⬇
investigate ideas
⬇
produce a specification
⬇
plan and make products
⬇
check quality
⬇
evaluate and test outcomes

Stages in design

What is a design brief?

A design brief is a statement that sets out the task to be solved. A design brief is usually quite short. A typical design brief could be:

> to design a savoury, **vegetarian** snack food which would appeal to teenagers and could be sold in a snack bar
>
> or
>
> to come up with ideas for a new winter soup.

When you analyse a design brief, pick out the **key words** or phrases. In the brief 'to design a savoury, vegetarian snack food which would appeal to teenagers and could be sold in a snack bar', the key words or phrases are savoury, vegetarian, snack, teenagers, sold in snack bar. These words are important if you want to meet the demands of the design brief.

Ways to gather research

If you were researching for the design of a vegetarian snack food you could follow these steps.

- Collect ideas from recipe books and magazines.
- Visit shops and snack bars, see what products

are sold and carry out an analysis.
- Carry out surveys and ask questions to find out what products people know and like.
- Ask experts such as dietitians or chefs for ideas.
- Look at existing products and examine the label and packaging information.

Produce a specification

A specification provides information about the product or products. The specification must meet the needs of the design brief. The range of vegetarian snack food could have the following specification.

- Must be suitable for vegetarians.
- **Portion** must be suitable for a snack but not a meal.
- Must appeal to teenagers.
- Must be savoury.
- Has to be able to be sold in a snack bar so must be reasonable price.

You could include other ideas of your own such as:

- must be able to be eaten in the hand
- must reheat well.

You could draw a star profile to show the design specification.

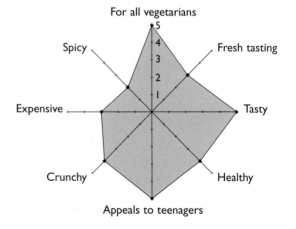

A star profile for a food product

A star profile is a graphical way of describing a food product. Each line on the star has a word or descriptor which describes the product. You then give each word a rating out of 5, where 0 = 'not' and 5 = 'very'. On the star profile on page 10, 'spicy' is given a rating of 2 out of 5, and 'tasty' is given a rating of 5 out of 5.

A detailed specification

When you have tasted and tested several ideas you are ready to give much more detail about the product you want to design. For the vegetarian product this could be:

- name and description of the product
- size and shape (include a drawing)
- ingredients and quantities to use
- appearance (colour, texture)
- how it is made (steps in the process)
- how long it will keep (with storage instructions).

See page 13 in the Teacher's Resource Pack for more information.

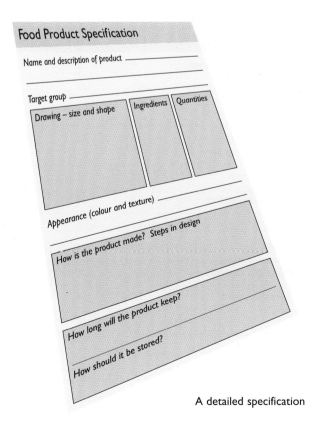

A detailed specification

Planning and making

Draw up plans for making the product. Include quality checks at each stage to make sure you end up with a product that looks attractive and is safe to eat. Test the result against the specification and see if it meets all the criteria.

In the chart below, which shows quality checks, one step has been completed as an example.

Steps	Quality checks
1 Collect and weigh ingredients.	1 Are the ingredients within their **date-mark** and safe to use?
	2 Are the ingredients weighed accurately?

Chart to show quality checks

Questions

Pick out the key words in each of the following design briefs. List a range of ideas that would match each brief.

1 Design a dessert which uses milk, or a milk-based product. The product should be suitable for a young child and be packed so that it is easy to eat.

2 Design a savoury snack that is suitable for teenagers to eat for a packed lunch or between meals.

3 Many people want to be able to buy single portions of food products. Design a savoury and a sweet product that could be suitable for an elderly person living on their own.

Getting information for research

You can carry out research in many ways.

Carrying out a survey

A survey is a list of questions that a range of people are asked, to find out their opinions and ideas. When design teams develop a new range of food products, they often use results of surveys to help them decide if there was a need for their new ideas. The charts on these pages come from a survey on teenage eating habits. A total of 1302 questionnaires were analysed. Almost equal numbers of boys (47 per cent) and girls (53 per cent) responded. The age profile of a survey is the age range of the group of people who took part.

Age (years)	%
under 12 years	5
12 years	20
13 years	24
14 years	28
15 years	17
over 15 years	6

The age profile of the students who took part

Meals and snacks

Most students ate lunch (93 per cent) and an evening meal (94 per cent) but a large number missed breakfast (22 per cent), particularly girls (30 per cent).

Snack foods

Meal/snack	Boys (%)	Girls (%)	Total (%)
breakfast	86	70	78
snack on the way to school	24	16	20
snack in the middle of the morning	56	59	57
lunch	95	91	93
snack on the way home from school	23	16	19
snack after school	72	65	69
evening meal	95	93	94
snack during the evening	53	39	46
snack before bed	60	47	53
snack in bed/ during the night	15	7	11

Meals and snacks eaten throughout the day

Snack foods

Foods/drinks	Boys (%)	Girls (%)	Total (%)
I don't eat between meals	5	5	5
crisps/savoury snacks	61	64	62
sandwich/toast/bread	39	35	37
cake/doughnut/ biscuit/Danish pastry	34	32	33
cereal and milk	27	15	20
fresh fruit/dried fruit	27	38	33
soup	13	8	10
yogurt	23	25	24
cheese and crackers	21	20	20
chocolate/sweets	57	54	55
nuts	13	10	11

Types of snacks eaten throughout the day

Other snack foods mentioned included pasta, pizza, popcorn, pot noodles, salad/raw vegetables, ice-cream, hot dogs, beans on toast, kebabs.

Take-away meals

Of the students in the survey, 40 per cent had a take-away meal at least once a day.

Take-away food	How often foods are eaten (%)					
	more than twice a day	once a day	5–6 times a week	2–4 times a week	once a week	none
Chinese/Indian meal	2	2	1	5	35	55
Kebab/burger/ hot dog	3	3	3	15	37	39
Fish and chips	4	4	3	14	47	29
Pizza	4	3	4	16	41	32
Portion of chips	5	8	6	22	36	22

The most popular take-away foods and how often they are eaten

Results of the survey carried out by the National Dairy Council with Youth Express *newspaper on teenage eating habits*

Questions

Use the survey results to answer the questions.

1 Which is the most popular:

a mealtime of the day

b snack time of the day for these students?

Explain in your own words why you think these meals and snack times are the most popular.

2 Which are the *three*:

a most popular

b least popular

snacks eaten by these students?

3 People are eating more take-away meals. According to this survey, what are the most popular take-away meals, and how often are they eaten each week?

4 Write a paragraph or draw up some charts to show how you would have answered the questions shown on the survey. Add questions that you would like to be answered.

5 Draw up your own survey to find out about eating habits of your age group.

Some teenagers enjoy snacks

To do

Imagine you are a member of a design team which has to come up with ideas for a new range of snack foods for teenagers. Decide when the snack food will be eaten. Make a list of ideas for food products. Use the survey results on these pages to support your work, then present a short report.

Disassembling food products

To disassemble something means to take it apart. You can disassemble existing food products by taking them apart to get ideas for design. Here are some questions you can ask to find out information.

Disassembly questions

Questions	Answers
What does the food product look like?	Describe its size, shape and colour.
What is its size?	Show weight, height, and length and a labelled drawing.
What is it made from?	Look at the list of ingredients. The largest ingredient comes first. The label may show the percentages of the main ingredients.
How long will it keep and how should it be stored?	Look at the date-mark and storage instructions.
How much does it cost and what is the cost for 100 grams?	Look at the label and work out the cost for 100 grams.
Who would buy it?	Discuss this with your group.
What is its nutritional value?	Look at the nutrition information on the label.
How should it be prepared and served?	Look at the instructions on the package.
How is it made?	Look carefully at the product and try and work out how you think it is made – you could write to the manufacturer for more information.
How much does each part of the product weigh?	Take the product apart and weigh the different sections.
What does it taste like?	Taste it and see!

To do

Look at this label for chocolate chip scones and try to answer some of the questions shown in the chart above.

Suitable for Home Freezing	Freeze on day of purchase. Use within 1 month.
To Defrost	Defrost in a cool dry place for 2 hours.

INGREDIENTS:
Wheat Flour, Water, Sugar, Vegetable Margarine, Plain Chocolate Chips (6%), Egg, Vegetarian Whey Powder, Salt.

SUITABLE FOR VEGETARIANS
STORE IN A COOL DRY PLACE AND ONCE OPENED IN AN AIRTIGHT CONTAINER.

QUALITY GUARANTEED:
We are happy to refund or replace any Tesco product which falls below the high standard you expect. Just ask any member of staff.
This does not affect your statutory rights.

Produced in the U.K. for Tesco Stores Ltd., Cheshunt EN8 9SL, U.K
© Tesco '94. 0730

5 018374 473738 >

NUTRITION

TYPICAL COMPOSITION	Each Scone (approx. 33g) provides	100 g (3½ oz) provide
Energy	523kJ/124kcal	1585kJ/377kcal
Protein	2.7 g	8.2 g
Carbohydrate	18.1 g	54.7 g
of which sugars	6.5 g	19.7 g
Fat	4.6 g	13.9 g
of which saturates	1.7 g	5.0 g
mono-unsaturates	2.2 g	6.7 g
polyunsaturates	0.6 g	1.7 g
Fibre	0.6 g	1.8 g
Sodium	0.2 g	0.5 g

This Pack contains 8 scones

INFORMATION

Label for chocolate chip scones

Scanning or photocopying food products

You can scan or photocopy cross-sections of food products to help record information. See page 27 for information about the use of photocopiers and scanners.

A scanned image of a scone

Why do food producers disassemble food products?

If a supermarket chain wants to design a new range of sandwiches, they might buy sandwiches from other supermarkets and sandwich shops. A design team then takes the product apart and looks at the different breads, spreads and fillings used. They measure the weight of each of the ingredients used to come up with their own ideas.

To do

Disassemble a range of ready meals or sandwiches.

You need
- 5 plates, 4 spoons, 3 knives, 2 electronic digital scales, 1 hygienic ruler

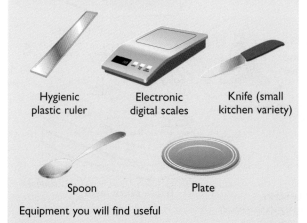

Hygienic plastic ruler   Electronic digital scales   Knife (small kitchen variety)

Spoon   Plate

Equipment you will find useful

Method
1 Draw up a chart to help analyse each product. The chart could be a series of questions or a form like the one shown opposite.

2 Disassemble the product. Start with the label and packaging information.

3 Take the product apart – measure it, weigh it, and work out the weight of the different sections.

4 Compare the results of other products in the range.

Note: Some products are difficult to disassemble in the classroom. You can work out the weight of ingredients in a ready-made salad, but you cannot work out the weight of ingredients in a cake or biscuit.

Questions

1 When a food manufacturer wants to develop a new range of food products, why does the design team buy other similar products and disassemble them? Give *three* reasons for your answer.

2 Use the label for chocolate chip scones and find the following information.

a How many scones are in the pack and how much does each scone weigh?
b What are the scones made from?
c How should the product be stored?
d Why are they suitable for vegetarians?

List the design ideas you get from this information.

3 Choose *one* of these food products: a sandwich, a pizza, biscuits, a pasta dish

a How would you disassemble this food product?
b List the information you want to find.
c How can you use this information to give you design ideas?

Design ideas

Create an image board

When design companies present new food product ideas, they sometimes make a **mood** or **image board** to show their clients. An image board is a display of pictures and drawings that show images relating to the food products. You can create your own image board by cutting out pictures from magazines and newspapers.

The image board below is for a new range of Mexican food products. It includes pictures of Mexican ingredients, plants that grow in the country, existing Mexican food products and colours that represent the country. Colourful image boards can help to give you design ideas and show why you have chosen certain ingredients for your food products. They can also help with package design.

An image board for a new range of Mexican food products

To do

Design an image board that shows ideas for one of the following food products:

a a range of Italian tomato sauces

b Indian vegetarian food

c a chocolate snack.

You need

- a sheet of A3 paper, scissors, glue, collection of magazines

Method

Look through the magazines and tear out any pictures that you think could identify with your product. Choose pictures of ingredients, people who might eat the product and other products which you could copy. Stick these pictures on the sheet of A3 paper.

Sketching and labelling ideas

A quick sketch of food product ideas with labels can show your design thinking. It can save you writing down ideas. This sketch shows labelled drawings for ideas for vegetarian snacks.

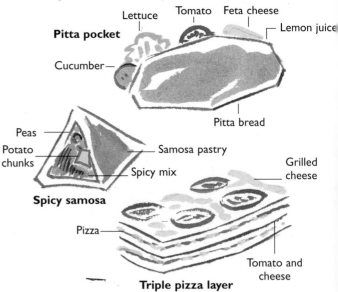

Vegetarian foods

If you are designing a range of products that are similar in shape, you could draw or scan in the image into the computer and then adapt the drawing to show design ideas. For example, if you were designing a range of speciality cakes, you could scan in the basic design then adapt it.

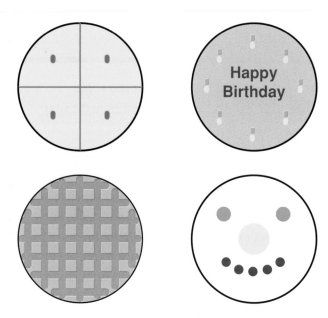

You can draw your ideas using a computer — these are ideas for cake icing

Concept screening

Concept screening is like putting design ideas through a sieve. The sieve sorts out which ideas can be used and keeps those that are suitable.

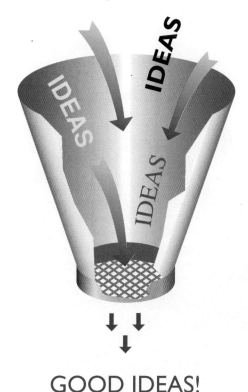

Concept screening

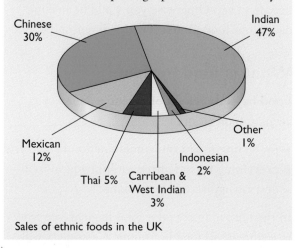

Did you know?

Mexican food is the fastest growing sector of the UK **ethnic food** market. Sales of products such as salsa, spicy Mexican tomato sauce and tortilla chips are increasing, and Mexican restaurants are opening up across the country.

Chinese 30%
Indian 47%
Mexican 12%
Thai 5%
Carribean & West Indian 3%
Indonesian 2%
Other 1%

Sales of ethnic foods in the UK

To do

Design a range of snack foods, with a Mexican image, that could be sold in a supermarket. Work in a group. Try to think up lots of ideas for this design brief. To screen your designs, take each idea and decide whether it might be worth developing further. You need some criteria to make the choices – for example, for each idea think about whether:

- most people will like it
- it will sell
- it is easy to make
- the idea is unusual and interesting.

Choose *three or four* ideas to develop and test further.

Questions

If you had to develop a range of snack foods from other countries, what areas of the world would you choose? Why? Use the pie chart above to help with your answer.

Food hygiene

Before you design and make any food product you need to know about food hygiene and find out how to prepare and store food so that it will be safe to eat. Otherwise you could be making dangerous food products that will poison people!

What is food hygiene?

Food hygiene is a set of practices aimed at keeping food clean by:

- protecting food from contamination by bacteria
- preventing bacteria from multiplying in food
- destroying bacteria by cooking.

In the food industry poor food hygiene can lead to outbreaks of food poisoning. Customers will complain, legal action may be taken, the business could be fined large amounts of money, and the business may even be forced to close down.

The owner of the Posh Nosh sandwich bar was fined £7500 for following a 130-year-old recipe using raw eggs to make mayonnaise. Sixty-two customers developed **salmonella** food poisoning and eight people had to go to hospital. The owner of the sandwich bar had used a recipe from *Mrs Beeton's Cookbook*, first published in 1861. The inspectors linked the food poisoning to the mayonnaise and told the man that he should know that raw eggs may contain salmonella bacteria and raw eggs should not be used in uncooked food products. He was found guilty of selling food unfit for human consumption.

Adapted from Daily Telegraph, *24 September 1994*

The Food Safety Act 1990 makes it an offence to sell food that is unsafe to eat, and people that work in the food industry must show due diligence (care) and do their best to make sure food is safe to eat.

The Food Safety (General Food Hygiene) Regulations 1995 require food businesses to assess the risks in making their food products and take action to make sure their food is safe. Food businesses must control and identify food **hazards** and put controls in place to reduce or eliminate these hazards. This **system** of controls is know as Hazard Analysis and Critical Control Point (HACCP).

Personal hygiene

In food preparation, personal hygiene refers to the way we keep ourselves clean and handle food to keep it safe to eat.

What hazards can you identify in this picture?

Handwashing

You use your hands a lot when working with food, so your hands must always be washed before touching food or equipment. Always wash your hands after using the toilet and after handling raw food, rubbish or cleaning materials. People working in the food industry must wash their hands with anti-bacterial soap and hot water before entering the food area.

Clothing

Wear clean, protective clothing for food preparation. This is to protect the food from contamination, and not to keep your clothes clean. In the food industry all workers wear special washable clothing, with no outside pockets. Hair must be completely covered, so workers wear hats and hair nets, and men even have nets for their beards.

Cuts

All cuts must be covered with waterproof plasters. Blue plasters are used by the food industry since they can be seen if they fall into food.

Food workers wear special clothing for their work

Hair and jewellery

Hair should be tied back for food work so that hairs do not fall into the food. Jewellery should be removed before working with food, as rings can hide dirt and bacteria.

Feeling sick?

If you feel sick or have diarrhoea, do not work with food until you are better. Dangerous bacteria could otherwise be passed onto food and cause food poisoning.

Smoking

In the food industry it is against the law to smoke when preparing food. Smokers can transfer harmful bacteria onto food when they touch their lips to remove a cigarette.

Food preparation areas

Keep food preparation areas very clean and clear from clutter. Wipe down the work surface with an anti-bacterial spray before starting to work with food. Workers in the food industry sterilize work surfaces regularly, using sanitizers.

Questions

1 What is meant by the following terms?

a   food hygiene
b   personal hygiene

2 What could happen if a food business did not have good food hygiene?

3 Why is it important for food workers:

a   to wash their hands before food work
b   to wear clean, protective clothing
c   to cover their hair
d   to cover cuts?

4 Why should you not work with food if you are sick?

5 Explain in your own words, the outbreak of food poisoning described in the newspaper article opposite.

Food safety

Food safety is essential to make sure food is safe to eat and to help prevent food poisoning.

Food poisoning

Bacteria are the most common cause of food poisoning. Bacteria are micro-organisms which cannot be seen without a microscope. Most bacteria are harmless. Many are useful such as those used to make cheese and yogurt.

Food-poisoning bacteria cause vomiting, diarrhoea, stomach cramps, fever and any combination of these symptoms. Some food-poisoning bacteria even cause death.

In the right conditions, bacteria can multiply by splitting in two every 10–20 minutes. In just 4–5 hours, one bacterium will have multiplied to many thousand.

For bacteria to grow and multiply the following four things are needed.

Warmth – Bacteria thrive at temperatures around 37°C – our body temperature. Bacteria will grow at any temperature between 5°C and 63°C. This temperature range is known as the **danger zone**. When working with food, try to keep the temperature of food above or below the danger zone to limit the time in which bacteria can multiply. Temperatures above 70°C will destroy most bacteria, so food should be cooked until it is **piping hot** – hotter than 70°C for two minutes.

Moisture – Bacteria need moisture (liquid) to grow, which is one reason why dried foods have a long **shelf life.** If foods have high levels of sugar (for example, jams), high levels of acid (for example, pickles) or salt (for example, salami) then the water in the foods is not available for the bacteria to grow.

Food – Bacteria prefer foods that are high in protein, and moist. These **high-risk foods** include meat, poultry, eggs and fish. High-risk foods also include mayonnaise and dairy products.

Time – Bacteria can multiply quickly in a very short time in the right conditions, so food must not be left in warm conditions for very long.

Danger points in food handling

The major danger points in food handling are:

- not cooking food properly
- preparing food too far in advance and keeping it at room temperature
- **cross-contamination** from raw to cooked food
- not thawing frozen food such as chicken properly
- not storing food in the refrigerator.

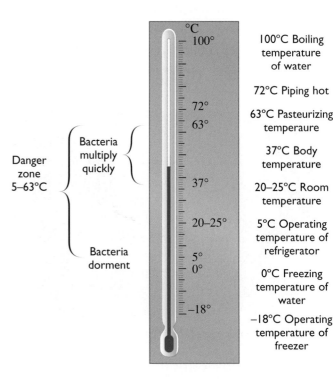

Food temperature chart

Poor temperature control is the most common cause of food poisoning – food may not be thoroughly cooked, food may be left in a warm room, or the refrigerator may not be working properly so the food is not kept cool.

Cross-contamination is the second most common cause of food poisoning. This means that ready-to-eat food is infected with bacteria from raw foods such as meat, from dirty tools and work surfaces or from people.

Using a food label

Food labels show 'use by' and 'best before' dates for food products, as well as storage and cooking instructions. Follow this information carefully. Scientists and food technologists have worked together to provide these instructions.

The label below shows the details for time and temperature in storing and cooking ready-to-eat tagliatelle.

See page 24 in the Teacher's Resource Pack for more information.

Use by time given

STORAGE

SUITABLE FOR HOME FREEZING
FREEZE ON DAY OF PURCHASE
USE WITHIN 3 MONTHS
DEFROST THOROUGHLY BEFORE USE

Storage time given

Food label for tagliatelle

Time and temperature given

COOKING

COOKING IN A CONVENTIONAL OVEN - PREHEAT OVEN TO 190°C, 375°F, GAS 5. REMOVE SLEEVE AND PIERCE FILM SEVERAL TIMES. PLACE ON A BAKING TRAY IN OVEN FOR 15 MINUTES. FOR **FAN ASSISTED OVENS** COOKING TIME SHOULD BE REDUCED BY APPROXIMATELY 3 MINUTES. FOR BEST RESULTS REFER TO MANUFACTURER'S HANDBOOK. **MICROWAVE COOKING** - MICROWAVE OVENS VARY. THE FOLLOWING RECOMMENDATION IS A GUIDE ONLY. REMOVE SLEEVE AND PIERCE FILM SEVERAL TIMES. PLACE POT IN OVEN AND COOK ON HIGH (100%). **FOR 750 WATT OR CATEGORY D OVENS** - 1½ MINUTES. **FOR 650 WATT OR CATEGORY B OVENS** - 2 MINUTES. ADJUST TIME ACCORDING TO YOUR PARTICULAR OVEN. AFTER COOKING LEAVE TO STAND FOR 1 MINUTE. REMOVE FILM AND STIR PRODUCT THOROUGHLY. **CHECK THAT PRODUCT IS HOT BEFORE SERVING.** TWO OR MORE PACKS WILL REQUIRE LONGER COOKING TIME. **DO NOT REHEAT.**

Preparing food for cooking

Raw foods such as fresh vegetables need to be prepared, to get them ready to eat. Vegetables may need washing and peeling; most can be eaten raw or cooked.

Preparing vegetables

Preparing vegetables

Method	Cabbage	Carrot	Onion
wash	✔		
scrub	✔		
peel	✔		
grate	✔		
slice	✔		
chop	✔		
chunk	✔		
leave whole	✗		
uncooked	coleslaw		
cooked	soup and stews		

To do

How would you prepare these vegetables for eating?

Tomato   Cucumber   Potato

Mushroom

Cabbage   Onion   Carrot

Draw up a chart like the one shown here. Tick the methods you could use for each vegetable. Suggest how the vegetables could be eaten raw (uncooked) and cooked. One example has been completed for you.

Tools for preparing vegetables

cook's knife

paring knife

grater

vegetable peeler

food processor

Tools to prepare vegetables

You need different tools to prepare the vegetables by different methods.

Tools	Chopping	Slicing	Peeling	Grating
cook's knife	✔	✔		
paring knife		✔	✔	
peeler			✔	
grater				✔
food processor	✔	✔		✔

Tools you can use for each method

Spoons for cooking

Different spoons that can be used for cooking include:

tablespoon, dessertspoon, teaspoon, measuring spoons, draining spoons, wooden spoons.

Tablespoon

Measuring spoons

Dessertspoon

Draining spoon

Teaspoon

Wooden spoon

Spoons used in cooking

To do

When would you use these spoons? Copy the chart and fill in your answers.

	Which spoon? – name it	Which spoon? – draw it
measuring		
mixing		
stirring		
eating		
serving food		

Cooking gadgets

Here are some gadgets that can be used to speed up food preparation and also to improve the accuracy of food production. There are other ways to make the food product without using gadgets.

Bread-making machine

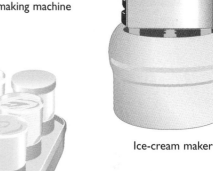

Ice-cream maker

Yogurt maker

Gadgets used in cooking

To do

Copy the chart below and complete it for each gadget. Can another method be used to make the product? Which method would give: **a** the quickest results **b** accurate results every time?

Gadget	Is there another way? – Describe it	Which method produces the quickest results?	Which method produces the most accurate results?
ice-cream maker			
bread-making machine			
yogurt maker			

Cooking methods

Why do we cook food?

Cooking food can:

- make food safer to eat, as dangerous bacteria are killed by heat
- add **flavour** and colour
- make food tasty and attractive.

Here are some of the methods of cooking that you can use to cook food.

Methods of cooking – microwave, roasting, steaming, frying, grilling

Method of cooking	How does it work?	Foods cooked by this method	Advantages
Baking	Food is cooked in an oven – heat passes around the oven by convection currents.	Bread, cakes, biscuits	Many foods have to be baked to give them their characteristic flavour and texture.
Roasting	Food is cooked in an oven with added fat. Some foods such as lamb and chicken already contain fat.	Meat, chicken, potatoes	Adds flavour and colour but increases fat content.
Grilling	Food is cooked under the grill by radiant heat.	Toast, sausages, bacon, tomatoes	Quick method of cooking, reduces fat content.
Frying	Food is cooked in a little or a lot of fat (deep fat frying). In dry frying, the food, such as bacon which contains some fat, is cooked without added fat.	Fish, chips, springs rolls, eggs	Quick method, gives flavour but adds extra fat.
Cooking in microwave	Microwave energy causes food molecules to vibrate, create heat and so cook food.	Reheating food, making sauces, cooking vegetables	Quick and cheap in fuel use.
Boiling/Stewing/ Poaching	Food is cooked in boiling water, usually in a saucepan.	Pasta, potatoes, rice, vegetables, eggs	Quite quick, no fat used.
Steaming	Food is cooked over steam from boiling water.	Vegetables, puddings, Chinese snacks	Quick, foods such as vegetables keep their crunchy texture.
Barbecuing	Food is cooked over wood or charcoal, often in open air.	Chicken, sweetcorn, sausages	Gives flavour and colour to food.

Cooking methods

Cooking in a microwave

An engineer called Percy Spencer made magnetrons used in radar systems which detected planes and ships during World War ll. He discovered that microwaves given out from a magnetron melted chocolate and popped the kernels of popcorn. The first microwave oven was produced in 1947, but it was large and expensive. The first domestic microwave was sold in 1967; now half the households in Britain own one. Vegetables are the most commonly microwaved foods.

Healthy fast food

Tandoori food is one of the healthiest options when it comes to fast food. In a *Daily Express* survey, tandoori chicken came out with the fewest calories compared to other fast foods such as pizza, fish and chips, McDonald's Big Mac and fries and a Chinese take-away.

A meal of tandoori chicken, mint dressing, side salad and a chapatti was voted the most health-conscious because little fat is used in the cooking, the mint dressing is yogurt-based and chapattis are usually made with wholemeal flour. All this adds up to only 479 calories for the average serving.

How other fast foods compare

Fish and chips	**1097 calories**
Big Mac and fries	**865 calories**
Sweet and sour pork with fried rice	**955 calories**
Cheese and tomato pizza	**570 calories**
Tandoori chicken	**479 calories**

Healthy Fast Food – Tandoori Magazine, *March 1996*

Cooking in a tandoor

A tandoor is a clay oven which is traditionally heated using burning charcoal. In India and Pakistan foods such as bread (nan), chicken and meat are cooked in a tandoor. The nan is cooked on the sides of the tandoor and pieces of chicken and meat are placed on skewers which are placed in the oven. Many Indian restaurants have tandoors for cooking.

A Shahi tandoor

Questions

1 Suggest *three* ways to cook each of these foods:

potatoes, eggs, sweetcorn, sausages, a slice of bread.

Add *three* more foods of your own to this list and suggest cooking methods.

2 Choose *one* of the foods and give the advantages and disadvantages of the three chosen cooking methods.

3 The article, 'Healthy fast food' compares the energy value of fast foods.

a Explain why Tandoori chicken has the lowest energy value (in other words the lowest number of calories).

b What cooking methods are used for each of the other foods?

c How does each cooking method affect the energy value of the food?

Equipment for food technology

Equipment such as food processors and mixers can speed up methods of making food products and also give accurate results when slicing and grating vegetables.

The food processor

Blade – used for grinding wheat to flour, blending vegetables for soup.

Attachments – used for slicing and grating vegetables, gives slices the same thickness.

Mixing attachment – a cake or scone mix can be mixed at the same speed and power each time, to achieve the same results.

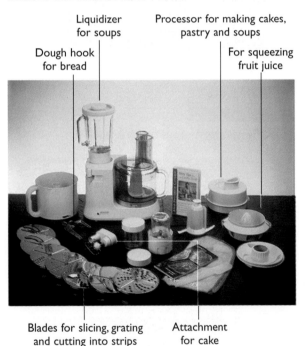

Dough hook for bread

Liquidizer for soups

Processor for making cakes, pastry and soups

For squeezing fruit juice

Blades for slicing, grating and cutting into strips

Attachment for cake

A food processor can provide a range of tools for food work

Accuracy

When you are designing and making food products, accuracy is important. You need special equipment that will help with accurate weighing and measuring, especially when you are disassembling a food product.

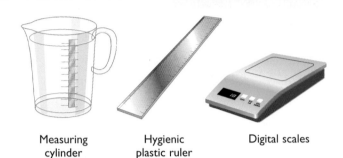

Measuring cylinder

Hygienic plastic ruler

Digital scales

Tools used in weighing and measuring

Weighing and measuring

Measuring cylinders – should be able to measure 5ml of liquid.

Metal or plastic rulers – can be used to measure the height and size of food products.

Digital electronic scales – help to measure food to an accuracy of 5 grams.

Tasting and testing

Tasting booth with equipment

Make a tasting booth and equip it with tasting pots, plates, spoons, labels, tasting charts and coloured lights.

yum...

A tasting booth

A food probe

Food probes – give accurate temperature measurements to within 1°C. When you taste hot food products, for a fair test, make sure they are all served at the same temperature. (Use anti-bacterial wipes to clean the probe each time it is used to prevent contamination.)

Recording results

A camera with a zoom lens is useful to photograph food products to keep a record of results.

Use a digital camera or video camera linked to a computer and import the results to show on the computer screen. The pictures can be printed when needed.

Use a photocopier or scanner to copy cross-sections of baked food products such as scones, bread and cakes. Make sure the food is covered with plastic film so that crumbs and grease do not get into the equipment.

A scanned cross-section of a scone

A dictaphone is useful to record thoughts and ideas as you work – the tape can be played back and used for written work.

A dictaphone

Questions

1 Make a list of the food processor attachments you can see on the photo opposite. Describe how each of the attachments can be used for food preparation. Give an example of a food which can be prepared using each of the attachments.

2 Explain how and why you would use the following equipment for food technology work:

a a tasting booth
b a food probe
c accurate digital scales.

Uses of food ingredients (1)

You need to know the uses (functions and properties) of ingredients when you make them into a food product. Ingredients have different functions and properties, depending upon how they are used in food products. Here are some examples of important ingredients used in cooking.

Uses of flour

Bulking ingredient – flour is the main ingredient in products such as bread, biscuits and cakes. It provides the mass or bulk.

Helps form the structure – the proteins in flour form the structure in baked goods such as bread and cakes.

Thickens liquids – the starch in flour swells when the flour is heated with a liquid to make a sauce or soup and so thickens the mixture.

Nutritious – flour provides starch, protein and dietary fibre (NSP), and vitamins and minerals.

Adds flavour, colour and texture – some flours such as wholemeal flour add a nutty flavour, a pale brown colour and crunchy texture.

Uses of eggs

Hold air – when beaten, eggs hold air, e.g. meringues.

Nutritious – eggs are good sources of protein, vitamins and minerals.

Setting and thickening – on heating, protein coagulates, sets and thickens, e.g. omelettes, cakes, egg sauces.

Coating food – eggs are used in batters and protect fried food.

Glazing – eggs are used to glaze pastry to make it golden when cooked.

Binding – eggs bind dry ingredients together in products such as fish cakes.

Emulsifier – helps to mix oil and water together, e.g. mayonnaise.

Eggs come in different sizes

Malted brown flour

Self-raising flour

Wholemeal flour

Plain flour

Softgrain flour

Pasta flour

Different flours

> **Word bank: uses of ingredients in food products**
>
> adds bulk, adds colour, adds flavour, adds texture, binding agent, emulsifier, holds air, makes food moist, nutritious, preservative, raising agent, sets food, shortening agent, structure, sweetener, thickens

Uses of fat

Fats include butter, margarine and oil.

Adds flavour – butter adds a special flavour to biscuits and cakes, and olive oil has a strong flavour.

Shortening agent – makes biscuits and cakes crumbly.

Increases the shelf life – baked goods are less dry.

Holds air – margarine helps hold air in cake mixtures.

Makes food moist – butter spread on bread makes food moist.

Different fats

Uses of sugar

Sugars include granulated, caster and icing sugar.

Sweetening agent – sweetens hot drinks and breakfast cereals.

Preservative – prevents food spoilage in jams and jellies.

Bulking agent – gives texture and volume to products such as cakes, ice-cream, icing and jams.

Speeds up fermentation – helps the reaction of yeast in bread-making.

Lightens cakes – when beaten with butter and eggs gives lightness and open texture.

Changes the flavour – softens the tartness of tomato sauces, and fruits such as grapefruit and gooseberries.

Lowers the freezing point – in ice-cream.

Different sugars

To do

Create your own word bank to show the uses (functions and properties) of food ingredients. For each word or phrase, give an example of an ingredient and its use in a food product, for instance, 'adds flavour – for example, using strawberries in a milk shake'.

Question

Use the word bank to explain the uses of the ingredients in each of the following food products.

a **flapjacks** made from oats, sugar, and golden syrup

b **pizza** with tomato and cheese topping

c **veggie burgers** made from beans, spices, beaten egg and onion

d **strawberry yogurt** made from yogurt, sugar and strawberries

You can present your work on a chart like the one shown below by identifying the use of each ingredient.

Flapjacks

Product ingredients	Use of each ingredient
oats	
sugar	
golden syrup	

Uses of food ingredients (2)

Many food products need to be thickened in some way. For example, a white sauce is thickened with flour or cornflour, soups can be thickened by starchy vegetables such as potatoes, and milk puddings can be thickened with rice or semolina.

Thickening food products

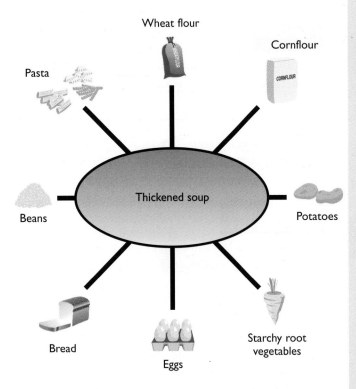

Wheat flour

Cornflour

Pasta

Beans

Thickened soup

Potatoes

Bread

Eggs

Starchy root vegetables

Spider chart to show the range of ingredients that can be used for thickening soup

For more detailed experimental work on how starch thickens liquids, see pages 17–19 in the Teacher's Resource Pack.

For more detailed experimental work on how starch thickens liquids, see pages 17–19 in the Teacher's Resource Pack.

To do

Investigate some food ingredients that can be used to thicken soup.

You need
- measuring jugs, saucepans, food processor, wooden spoon, small knife, tasting spoons, bowls

Food ingredients
carrots, potatoes, turnip, parsnip, yam, sweet potato, bread, canned butter beans, lentils, pasta, noodles, stock cubes, boiling water

Method

1 Work in pairs to design and make one thickened soup.

2 Choose 100 grams of one of the food ingredients (peeled weight). Chop up root vegetables such as carrots and potatoes into small pieces.

3 Put a stock cube into a measuring jug and make up to 500 ml with boiling water.

4 Pour into a saucepan and add 100 grams of food ingredients to the stock. Cook on a low heat until the ingredients are soft – no more than 10 minutes.

5 Make a note of the thickness of your soup. You could rate the thickness level as follows: 3 = very thick, 2 = quite thick, 1 = not very thick. Blend the soup in a food processor until it is smooth. Present your soup in a bowl. Compare the result with those of others.

6 Taste the range of soups and compare the results for thickness.

7 Evaluate the results of the tasting.

a Which ingredients are used to thicken soups?
b What happened when you blended the soup in a processor – does it make the soup thicker?

8 Comment on your results.

Design a soup

There are many reasons why ingredients are chosen for soup making – for example, flavour, colour, texture.

To do

Design a soup and make a list of the ingredients you want to use. Explain why you have chosen the ingredients for your soup, showing the use of each ingredient in the soup recipe. What alternative ingredients could you use if each of the ingredients was not available?

Thickening food products with starch

Flour and cornflour are starch-based food products which are often used to thicken liquids to make sauces and soups.

Heat starch granules in water

Starch granules become swollen

Starch granules burst

The liquid thickens and gelatinizes

Starch grains thicken sauces and soups

How does starch thicken a liquid?

When starch is heated in water, the water passes through the walls of the starch granules, they become swollen and burst. By this process the starch absorbs water and thickens the liquid. This process is known as gelatinization.

Experimental work

You can experiment and compare the thickening properties of flour, cornflour and other starchy foods. You can also find the best methods to thicken a liquid using these starches. The results of the research will help you design and make thickened sauces and soups. You can decide upon the type and quantity of the starch product to use and the stages in the process to make the sauce or soup.

Word bank: the texture of sauces

creamy, foamy, lumpy, powdery, runny, slimy, smooth, soggy, sticky, thick, thin, watery

Questions

1 For each word in the word bank, think of a product that would meet this descriptor. For example: watery – school soup!

2 What starchy foods are used to thicken each of the following products?

a rice pudding   **b** tapioca pudding

c blancmange   **d** cheese sauce

e packet mix custard   **f** gravy powder

Uses of food ingredients (3)

One of the most important uses of ingredients in a food product is to add flavour.

These pages look at how to design a tomato sauce for pasta, and focus on developing the flavour.

> ## Word bank: flavour
>
> bitter, delicious, fruity, herby, salty, sour, spicy, sweet

What is flavour?

To do

Carry out a tasting session of tomato sauces which are for sale. Choose sauces that are canned, bottled, chilled and dried. Prepare them according to instructions and carry out a tasting session. During the tasting, think of words to describe the looks, flavour and texture of the sauces. These words are **sensory descriptors**. You can compare the results using a star profile. Put the sensory descriptors onto the lines of the star and give them a rating of 0–5, where 0 = 'not' and 5 = 'very'. For more help see page 29 in the Teacher's Resource Pack.

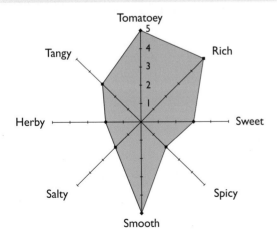

Star profile showing the sensory descriptors for a tomato sauce for pasta

Case study

Roz Denny

Designing a tomato sauce for pasta

Roz Denny, the food designer, was given the brief to design a range of high quality sauces for pasta, based upon tomatoes and using natural ingredients. The sauce had to taste home-made, would be sold in jars, stored at room temperature, and sell for about £1.50.

The first ideas she presented to the food company were descriptions, not recipes. For example, 'chunky tomato with a high degree of oil, pieces of basil, green pepper and chopped olives which could be poured over pasta'.

The company selected some of her ideas to be developed as concept samples. These are like a recipe for four people, and everything must be weighed and described exactly. Roz presented her recipes for a tasting session and the company chose the recipes that might be made in a factory.

The production department in the factory had to find large quantities of the ingredients that Roz used and match them in flavour, colour and texture. If some ingredients were too expensive, such as extra virgin olive oil, then a substitute had to be found with a similar flavour – in this case using less olive oil.

The sauce was made, and then tested by a large number of the public at a hall test (carried out in a large hall!). This development took nine months, and then the sauces were ready to go on sale.

Designing for flavour

To do

Design and make your own tomato sauce for pasta.

- Write a sentence to describe the sauce you want to make.
- List the sensory descriptors for your sauce and draw a star profile.
- List the ingredients you could use to meet each of these tastes. The chart below will help you.
- Find a basic tomato sauce recipe to adapt.
- Test out your ideas and taste the results.
- Work out an exact recipe that meets your tastes.
- Serve the sauce with boiled pasta.
- How will your sauce will be packaged for sale – fresh, frozen, canned, bottled, dried? Give reasons for your choice.

Tomato sauce for pasta

Ingredients

chopped tomatoes, tomato purée, water, vegetable oil, sugar, starch, onions, salt, paprika, herbs, garlic, chilli

---

Sensory descriptors	Choice of ingredients
tomatoey	fresh or canned tomatoes, tomato purée
salty	salt
sweet	tomatoes, sugar
herby	basil, oregano, parsley
spicy	paprika, pepper, garlic, chilli
tangy	tomatoes
smooth	(use a food processor)
rich	butter or oil

Sensory descriptors for tomato sauce

Tomato sauce for pasta recipe which can be adapted

Ingredients

1 medium onion finely chopped, 1 diced carrot, 1 crushed clove garlic, 2 tbs olive oil, 1 400-gram can chopped tomatoes, salt, pepper, sugar, fresh chopped basil.

Method

Fry the onion, carrot and garlic in the oil until they are soft. Add the tomatoes, salt, pepper, and sugar. Cook for 5 minutes, then purée in a food processor. Serve with chopped basil.

Did you know?

A food producer must make sure that the company's tomato sauce tastes the same throughout the year, despite variations in the weather and the time of year. A large-scale specification for the ingredients for tomato sauce includes:

- details of the type of tomatoes to be used, with their acidity and sweetness level
- the size of the granules of salt and sugar to be used
- details of the flavours of the herbs – a frozen sample is kept to make sure the flavour is the same
- the type of water to be used.

For more information see page 13–14 in the Teacher's Resource Pack.

Questions

1 What are the stages a food designer might follow when designing a tomato sauce?

2 Why does the large-scale manufacturer need a detailed specification for tomato sauce?

Nutrients

Food labels show nutrition information for the food products. What is the function of each of the nutrients shown on a full nutrition food label?

Note: The full nutrition label shows energy, protein, carbohydrate (of which sugars), fat (of which saturates), fibre and sodium.

Energy

Energy is needed for activity and to help the body function. Energy that is provided by food is measured in two ways:

- in calories, written as kcal
- in joules, written as kJ.

One kcal (calorie) is roughly equal to four kJ.

Energy is needed for activity

Nutrition information		
	Typical values	
	per 100 g	**per serving**
Energy	312 kJ/75 kcal	655 kJ/158 kcal
Protein	4.7 g	9.9 g
Carbohydrate	13.6 g	28.6 g
of which sugars	6.0 g	12.6 g
Fat	0.2 g	0.4 g
of which saturates	0.1 g	0.2 g
Fibre	3.7 g	7.8 g
Sodium	0.5 g	1.1 g

A full nutrition label

Example and information taken from Foodsense, Use your label: making sense of nutrition information *(Ministry of Agriculture, Fisheries and Food, MAFF)*

Protein

Protein is needed by the body for growth and repair. In the UK most adults eat more protein in food than they need. Foods that provide plenty of protein include meat, fish, poultry, eggs, cheese, beans and seeds.

Carbohydrates

Carbohydrates are made up mainly of sugars and starch. Carbohydrates are used to provide energy, but if we eat more carbohydrate than we need, the excess carbohydrate is stored as body fat.

Starch

We should get most of our energy in the form of calories, from starch instead of from fats and sugars. Foods that provide plenty of starch include bread, pasta, rice, breakfast cereals and potatoes.

Sugar

On a food label, 'sugars' means all types of sugar including those which occur naturally in fruit and milk, and added sugar, which is table sugar. Added sugar, if eaten often, can cause tooth decay.

Fat

Health experts suggest that we cut down on the amount of fat that we eat, especially foods containing saturated fat. High intakes of fat are linked to health problems and can lead to obesity (overweight). Fats are concentrated sources of energy, and many fats contain vitamins A and D which are important for good health.

The three main types of fat are saturates, monounsaturates and polyunsaturates.

Saturated fat – may raise blood cholesterol levels which may cause heart disease. Saturated fats are found in meat products such as pies and sausages, dairy produce, and cakes and biscuits made from hydrogenated vegetable oil or butter. Some food labels tell you how much of the total fat is from saturates. Some labels show the amount of monounsaturates and polyunsaturates. Most foods are mixtures of saturates, monounsaturates and polyunsaturates.

Monounsaturates – are not associated with heart disease and are found in olive oil and rape seed oil.

Polyunsaturates – lower blood cholesterol levels and are found in sunflower oil and soya oil.

Dietary fibre

Dietary fibre helps to prevent constipation, piles and bowel problems. Dietary fibre is found in foods that come from plants. Good sources of dietary fibre include baked beans, high-fibre breakfast cereals, wholemeal bread and fruit and vegetables.

Sodium

Most of the sodium in food comes from salt, which is added to food products such as sausages and cheese. Sodium has been linked with high blood pressure.

Vitamins and minerals

We only need vitamins and minerals in very small amounts, but they are essential to keep us fit and healthy. If details of vitamins and minerals are shown on food labels, they must be present in a 'significant amount', according to government guidelines.

Vitamins can be water soluble (vitamin C and the B group) or fat soluble (vitamins A, D, E and K). Minerals that are important for our health include calcium (for bones and teeth) and iron (needed for a healthy blood system).

Questions

1 Why are the following nutrients important in our diet?

a protein
b carbohydrate
c fat
d dietary fibre (not strictly a nutrient)

2 List *two* foods that are good sources of each nutrient.

3 What problems have been linked with high intakes of saturated fat?

4 What is the difference between saturated, monounsaturated and polyunsaturated fat?

Healthy eating

Following a healthy diet, taking more exercise and not smoking are all important factors in achieving a healthy lifestyle. These are the eight 'Healthy eating guidelines' from the government.

- Enjoy your food.
- Eat lots of different foods.
- Eat the right amount to stay a healthy weight.
- Eat plenty of foods rich in starch and fibre.
- Don't eat too much saturated fat.
- Don't eat sugary foods too often.
- Look after the vitamins and minerals in your foods.
- If you drink alcohol, keep within sensible limits.

The Balance of Good Health

The 'Balance of Good Health' is based upon the eight guidelines above. A balance of foods should be consumed for a healthy diet. We should choose foods from the following five food groups.

Bread, other cereals and potatoes – these are good sources of starch, and about a third of the food we eat should come from this group.

Fruit and vegetables – aim to eat at least five servings a day.

Milk and dairy foods – eat moderate amounts of these foods and choose lower fat alternatives.

Meat, fish and alternatives – eat moderate amounts of these foods and choose lower fat alternatives.

Fatty and sugary foods – eat them in small amounts and not too often.

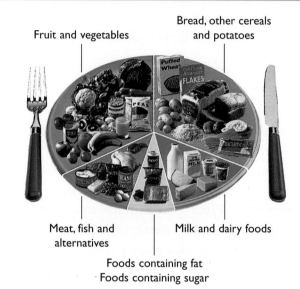

Fruit and vegetables

Bread, other cereals and potatoes

Meat, fish and alternatives

Milk and dairy foods

Foods containing fat
Foods containing sugar

The 'Balance of Good Health' (The Health Education Authority)

Healthy eating symbols on food products

Food companies are using special symbols on food products which meet healthy eating criteria.

Sainsbury's 'Healthy eating' symbol

Sainsbury's 'Healthy eating' symbol is found on foods which are generally low in fats and have a limited amount of added sugar and sodium (salt).

Tesco's 'Healthy eating' symbol

Tesco has a 'Healthy eating' product range which has been developed to be lower in fat and saturated fat, higher in fibre, and to provide the right balance of sugar and salt.

Nutrition and food design

Many food products are designed to meet specific nutritional needs. Some Marks & Spencer food products have symbols which show the amount of fat, energy and fibre in the products. They include:

Fat free – total fat content is less than 0.15 g per 100 g

Less than 300 cals – for people who may be watching their weight

Low fat – total fat is less than 5 g per normal serving

Reduced fat – fat content is at least 25 per cent less than the regular product

Lite – a reduced calorie product, total energy is at least 25 per cent less than regular product

High-fibre – foods contain at least 6 g of fibre.

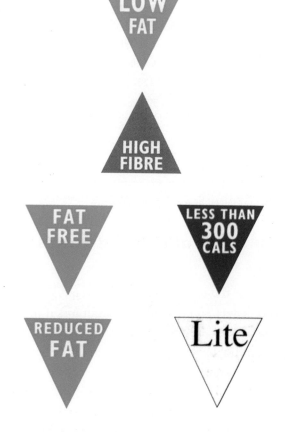

Marks & Spencer's 'Healthier choice' symbols

A lot: these amounts or more		A little: these amounts or less	
10 g	of sugars	2 g	of sugars
20 g	of fat	3 g	of fat
3 g	of fibre	0.5 g	of fibre
0.5 g	of sodium	0.1 g	of sodium

Guidelines for a complete main meal, or 100 grams of a snack food

These guidelines have been given in a booklet, Foodsense, Use your label: making sense of nutrition information, *published by the Ministry of Agriculture, Fisheries and Food (MAFF). © Crown copyright.*

Questions

1 Look at the nutrition information for the food products listed below. For each one, state whether they contain:

(i) a lot (ii) a little (iii) in between 'a lot' and 'a little' of:

a sugars
b fat
c fibre
d sodium.

Food products

> **Tagliatelle with ham per 100g:** 1.2 g of sugar, 6 g of fat, 0.9 g of fibre, 0.31 g of sodium

> **Cheese rolls per 100 g:** 1.9 g of sugar, 14.2 g of fat, 3.5 g of fibre, 0.6 g of sodium

> **Apple sponge per 100 g:** 13 g of sugar, 10.5 g of fat. 0.4 g of fibre, 0.1 g of sodium

> **Bacon and cheese burgers per 100 g:** 3.6 g of sugar, 21 g of fat, 2.2 g of fibre, 0.5 g of sodium

2 Suggest what foods you would serve with each of these products to make a two-course meal which meets the 'Healthy eating guidelines'.

Nutrition labelling

When you design and make a food product, you may want to create a label to show the nutritional information for the product. Nutrition information is not required yet on food products unless a nutritional claim about the product is made. If the nutritional information is shown, food labelling rules permit the following two standard lists of nutrients.

Basic label – with a minimum list of four nutrients.

Full label – with a detailed list of eight nutrients.

Nutrition information	Typical values
	per 100g
Energy	312 kJ
	75 kcal
Protein	4.7 g
Carbohydrate	13.6 g
Fat	0.2 g

Basic label for biscuits

Nutrition information	Typical values	
	per 100g	per portion
Energy	312 kJ	655 kJ
	75 kcal	158 kcal
Protein	4.7 g	9.9 g
Carbohydrate	13.6 g	28.6 g
of which sugars	6.0 g	12.6 g
Fat	0.2 g	0.4 g
of which saturates	0.1 g	0.2 g
Fibre	3.7 g	7.8 g
Sodium	0.5 g	1.1 g

Full label for biscuits

Foodsense, Use your label: making sense of nutrition information © *Crown copyright*

The nutrition content must be shown per 100 grams, but many labels also have information per serving. If serving information is given, the weight or portion size also has to be given.

How much is a serving?

A half-can serving of baked beans weighs just over 200 grams, so a serving gives twice the amount of nutrients listed per 100 grams on the nutrition label.

On some nutrition labels you will get extra information showing figures for starch, monounsaturates, polyunsaturates, cholesterol, vitamins and minerals.

Baked beans

Working out the nutrition label for a food product

First decide whether you want to create a basic label or a full label. You will need an exact recipe (formulation) for your food product, with quantities of the ingredients. Use food tables or a nutritional computer program to look up the nutritional value of each ingredient. Add up the total nutritional information for the whole recipe.

PIZZA
Bacon and Tomato

Label from food list   Pizza
Total cooked weight   580 g
Number of portions   3

Nutrition information – Pizza		
	Typical values	
	per 100 g	**per serving**
Energy	1287 kJ	2487 kJ
	307 kcal	594 kcal
Protein	9.68 g	18.7 g
Carbohydrate	22.6 g	43.6 g
Fat	20.5 g	39.6 g

A label produced by a computer program

How much of each nutrient is there in 100 grams?

Work out the total weight of the recipe. (You could deduct 10 per cent for weight loss if the recipe is cooked.) Divide the weight of each nutrient by the total weight and multiply by 100 to get the amount per 100 grams.

$$\text{Nutrient per 100 grams} = \frac{\text{total amount of nutrient}}{\text{total product weight}} \times 100$$

How much per portion?

Decide how many people the product serves. A pizza may serve two people. To find the amount per portion divide the total nutrients in the whole product by the number of portions.

Nutritional value per portion of pizza $=\dfrac{\text{total nutritional value of pizza}}{\text{number of portions made}}$

This example shows how to work out the nutrition information for a Basic label.

Summer pudding made from soft summer fruits

Step 1

Sort out the exact amount of ingredients for the recipe and know how many portions the recipe will serve.

Strawberry and raspberry summer pudding recipe (serves 8)

500 g strawberries
250 g raspberries
100 g caster sugar
8 slices white bread (30 g each slice) = 240 g

Step 2

Work out the nutritional analysis for the recipe.

Step 3

Use this information for the basic label to include values per 100g and per serving.

	Typical values per 100 g	Per serving 136 g
energy	435 kJ/102 kcal	592.5 kJ/139 kcal
protein	2 g	3 g
carbohydrate	23 g	3 g
fat	0.4 g	0.5 g

Nutrition chart for summer pudding

Food	Energy		Protein g	Carbohydrate g	Fat g
	kJ	kcal			
500 g strawberries	565	135		4	30
250 g raspberries	273	62.5		3.5	11.5
100 g sugar	1680	394		0	100
240 g bread	2222	521		18	112
total weight = 1090g	4740	1113		25.5	253.5
per 100 g	435	102		2	23
weight per portion = 136 g (approximately)	592.5	139		3	32

Chart to show nutrition information calculations for a summer pudding

Source: Food Tables, *McCance and Widdowson*

To do

1 Describe two ways that the information found on a nutrition label can be used by people.

2 Set up a spreadsheet to work out the nutritional information for the summer pudding. Your results should match those shown above. Use a computer program to work out the nutritional analysis for this product and compare results. See page 48 in the Teacher's Resource Pack for information.

Writing a specification for a food product

The final specification for a food product gives exact details of the product so that it can be made again with the same results. A food specification can include details of:

- product name
- size, shape and weight of the product
- ingredients used
- how long it will keep and how it will be stored
- appearance
- details of how the product is made.

Chocolate chip muffins

(Recipe name – product name) Makes 12

Ingredients (in order of use in recipe)
200 g self raising flour
1 teaspoon ground cinnamon (3 g)
40 g soft brown sugar
50 g chocolate chips
1 size 3 egg (60 g)
250 ml milk
2 tablespoons sunflower oil (30 ml)

Special equipment
12 paper baking cases

Method (step by step)
1 Set the oven at Gas Mark 5/190°C. Put the baking cases into a 12-hole bun tin.

2 Sieve the flour and cinnamon into a bowl and mix in the sugar and chocolate chips.

3 Beat the egg in a measuring jug and add the milk and the oil. Quickly stir into the flour mixture and beat thoroughly.

4 Spoon into the paper cases and bake in the centre of the oven for 15 minutes until well risen and brown.

5 The muffins are best eaten warm.

Source: Children's fun to cook book *by Roz Denny and Caroline Waldegrave*

To do

Making muffins
Use the recipe for chocolate chip muffins to write a specification for the product using the details for a specification listed opposite.

Tip: To work out the weight of each muffin:

- add up the total weight of the ingredients
- take off 10 per cent of this weight to allow for cooking loss
- divide the result by 12 (the total number of muffins made) to give the weight of each muffin.

Note: The recipe includes the exact cooking temperature and baking time.

❶ Set the oven

Put in baking cases

❷ Sieve the flour

3   Mix egg, oil and milk

4   Put in baking cases

5   Bake

Making the muffins step by step

A food label from a pack of muffins

INGREDIENTS

WHEAT FLOUR, SUGAR, WHOLE EGG, PLAIN CHOCOLATE CHIPS, VEGETABLE OIL (WITH ANTIOXIDANT:E321, E330), WATER COCOA POWDER, MODIFIED WHEAT STARCH, WHEY POWDER, RAISING AGENTS: 500, 541; WHEAT STARCH, EMULSIFIERS: E477, E471, E322.; SALT, WHEAT GLUTEN, FLAVOURS, STABILIZER: E415

The Sunbrite Guarantee: This product should reach you in perfect condition. If you are not satisfied, return the label to Sunbrite indicating when the product was purchased. This does not affect your statutory rights.

Sunbrite Bakeries Ltd.
Sheffield Lane, Rotherham R6 2LS

5 010156 411374

American style

4

Double Chocolate Chip
MUFFINS

Drawing a flow diagram

A flow diagram is a series of steps to show the process of making a product. You can draw these steps in boxes, or as a list of steps – for example, Step 1, Measure ingredients. See pages 48–49 for more information.

Questions

1 If the recipe for Chocolate chip muffins were to have a food label, the ingredients would be listed in descending order of weight with the largest quantity first. List the ingredients for the chocolate chip muffins as they would be shown on a food label.

2 The food label shows the ingredients used for Double chocolate chip muffins that are made on a large scale in a bakery. Compare the ingredients used in the recipe opposite with those used for the large-scale recipe. You could use a chart like the one shown below. Explain why you think the large-scale recipe has different ingredients.

Ingredients for small scale	Ingredients for large scale
self-raising flour	wheat flour

3 Draw a flow diagram to show how the muffins are made and show what safety and quality checks are needed at each stage.

Writing a recipe

A recipe usually includes a list of ingredients and a method. In industry, a recipe may be called a **formulation**. A recipe should be clear and easy to follow, so that people can make the food product without needing extra help. In large-scale food manufacture, recipes must provide precise information so that the product can be made time and time again.

These recipes for Green fingers and Lentil cutlets come from *Vegan Recipes* by Fay Henderson published in 1946. The recipes are in old measures, and need to be converted to **metric measures.**

Guidelines on recipe-writing

- Give the recipe a title.
- State how many people the recipe will serve.
- List the ingredients in order of use.
- Give the exact weight or size, and a description of the ingredients – for example, 50 grams caster sugar.
- Give the oven temperature and cooking time.
- Prepare the ingredients in order.
- Explain any difficult food terms (such as sauté or simmer) clearly.

Green fingers

Windfall apples, wholemeal pastry, fresh sweet herbs, sugar

Pulp the apples and sweeten to taste.

Line a sponge tin with pastry and spread the apple pulp over it.

Make a collection of fresh sweet herbs, such as mint, balm, thyme, elderflower. Wash and drain, snip up finely over the apple and cover the top with pastry. Cook in a quick oven until crisp and brown. Cut into fingers and serve cold.

Lentil cutlets

Soak ½ lb (half a pound) of red lentils overnight, then tie them in a muslin bag. Cover with cold water and boil slowly for 20 minutes. Empty into a hot dish and quickly add 1 oz of grated Suenut (a vegan suet), minced onion, finely snipped parsley and salt and pepper. Mix well together and shape into cutlets, covering with fine breadcrumbs and bran. Place in a hot dish in the oven and serve either hot with tomato sauce made from the liquid, or cold with sliced tomato.

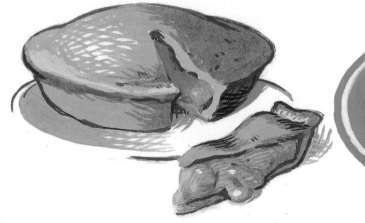

Green fingers

Lentil cutlets

Metrication

If you are using old recipe books to help with research for food ideas, you will find that the ingredients are given in **imperial measures.** For more than 20 years British recipes have been given in imperial and metric units, but now that ingredients are sold in metric units, it makes sense to use metric units for recipes. Food producers use metric units for product design. Electric ovens have been regulated in Celsius for many years.

What are metric units?

Weight measurements are in grams (g) and kilograms (kg). Volume and liquid measures are in millilitres (ml) and litres(l). Length is measured in millimetres (mm), centimetres (cm) and metres (m).

Note:

1000 g = 1 kilogram
1000 ml = 1 litre
1000 mm = 1 metre

How to measure in metric

Most scales, measuring jugs and rulers carry both metric and imperial measurements. The Guild of Food Writers has produced a leaflet, 'Metric Made Easy'. They suggest that if you are using an old recipe with imperial measures, you don't convert them into metric. Instead, use the dual measuring scales and jugs and measure the ingredients using the imperial system. You can then read the metric version from the scales.

Spoon sizes

The capacities of metric spoons are 5 ml, 10 ml and 15 ml. These measures are nearly the same as teaspoons, dessertspoons and tablespoons.

Weight/solids		Volume/liquids	
metric	imperial	metric	imperial
15 g	½ oz	15 ml	½ fl oz
25 g	1 oz	30 ml	1 fl oz
40 g	1½ oz	50 ml	2 fl oz
50 g	1¾ oz	100 ml	3½ fl oz
75 g	2¾ oz	125 ml	4 fl oz
100 g	3½ oz	150 ml	¼ pint
125 g	4½ oz	200 ml	⅓ pint
150 g	5½ oz	300 ml	½ pint

Chart to show some metric and imperial measures

The Guild of Food Writers metrication leaflet

Questions

Use the recipes for Green fingers and Lentil cutlets opposite to answer the questions.

1 These recipes were written over 50 years ago. Suggest the improvements that could be made so that they meet each of the points from the *Guidelines on recipe-writing* listed opposite. Try to rewrite these recipes in line with the guidelines.

2 List the words and phrases that you find difficult to understand and find out their meanings.

3 Why would food producers find these recipes difficult to use if they were making large quantities of these recipes?

4 Why do you think it is important that we change recipes to metric measures?

Food systems and control

What is a system?

A system is made up of four stages: input, process, output and **feedback**. The input starts the system, the process is the way the system changes, the output is the end result and the feedback is used to control the system by checking that the output is what is needed. Making a cake is a system.

- The input is the ingredients for the cake.
- The process is mixing and baking the cake.
- The output is a baked cake – the changes the system brings to the finished product.
- The feedback is to test if the cake is properly cooked and a good quality. If not, changes in the system are needed such as baking the cake for longer.

When making any food product, systems need to be controlled, to make sure that the product is safe to eat and of good quality.

Input – ingredients

Process – mixing and baking

Output – baked cake

Cake-making as a system

Temperature control – during food storage, cooking and serving	**Quality control** – throughout the process to make sure the product meets quality standards
Process control – controlling steps in the making process such as weighing ingredients and cutting food accurately	**Foreign body control** – making sure that no metal or dirt gets into food products
Hygiene and safety controls – to ensure safe working practice and safe food products	**Taste, nutrition and cost control** – constant checks are needed to make sure food meet the specification nutrition and cost

Chart to show controls in food product development

The difference between quality assurance and quality control

Quality assurance systems rely heavily on the expertise of food managers in identifying in advance where problems are likely to occur and setting up formal control systems to stop them happening. Quality assurance systems are replacing quality control as a concept.

If quality controls are used on their own, faults are only identified after the product has been made, and then it must be either reworked or wasted.

Institute of Food Science and Technology

Control	How to use control systems in food technology at school	How control systems are used in the food industry
Temperature control	Temperature can be measured using food probes which can be inserted into food products during storage, cooking and reheating.	Temperature sensors which are linked to computers monitor the changes in temperature and alert people to changes which might affect the quality of the product, such as the biscuit oven temperature dropping too low.
Quality control	You can set up a series of checks throughout the making process to make sure that the quality standards are met.	Quality assurance procedures are set up before the product is made and regular checks made throughout production.
Hygiene and safety controls, process control	Make sure you work hygienically and safely with food, checking that you follow the making process exactly.	The workforce is trained in hygiene and safety procedures, and checked to see that they follow these methods.
Foreign body control	Look at food and check food to make sure there is no dirt or unwanted material in it.	Metal detectors check food at the end of production to see if there are unwanted metal objects in food; workers look and check to make sure that raw ingredients are clean.
Taste, nutrition and cost control	Carry out tastings, nutritional and cost analysis.	Food is tasted to make sure it meets the standards set, computer programs check nutritional values and product costs.

Using control systems in food production

Question

Complete a system chart for making each of the following food products.

a   a sandwich
b   biscuits
c   making a hot drink

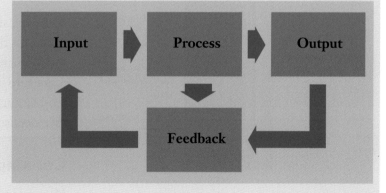

Temperature control

Temperature control is essential throughout the food production process both at home and for the food industry. It is important to limit the time that food spends in the danger zone – between 5°C and 63°C – so that dangerous bacteria do not multiply.

Temperature control is needed at all these stages of storing and making food products:

- buying food
- storing food in freezers and refrigerators
- making food products
- cooking in ovens and microwave cookers
- keeping food warm
- cooling food down
- storing in freezers and refrigerators
- reheating.

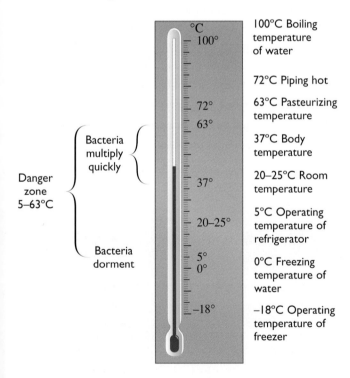

This thermometer shows the danger zone temperatures

Buying food

Use a cool bag when shopping for food to keep perishable food cool. Store perishable food as soon as possible after shopping to stop the temperature from rising.

Storing food

In the freezer food should be stored at –18°C. The freezer temperature can be monitored with a freezer thermometer.

The refrigerator should operate at 5°C or below. Perishable food should be kept cool at 8 °C.

Use a refrigerator thermometer to measure the temperature and insert a food probe into the food to measure the food temperature.

Making food products

Try to make food products quickly – do not leave food in a warm room. Cook food as soon as it is ready, or store it in the refrigerator.

Cooking in ovens and microwave cookers

The oven should be tested to make sure food is cooked at the correct temperature. Use an oven thermometer and test the food with a probe to make sure it is thoroughly cooked. Cooking food in microwave cookers needs special care. (See opposite.)

Cooking food

Meat and poultry dishes should be cooked to a temperature of 70°C for two minutes in different parts of the food.

Keeping food warm

Hot food must be kept at a temperature of at least 63°C or above to stop bacteria from multiplying. The temperature must be checked at regular intervals, using a food probe.

Cooling food down

If you want to cool food for storage or to reheat later, try to cool it as quickly as possible. Cut large portions of food such as chicken into smaller quantities, spread cooked food such as rice onto large trays and place in a cool place. When the food is cool, cover it and store it in the refrigerator. Do not put warm food straight into refrigerators or freezers as this will cause a rise in temperature.

Reheating food

Only reheat food once, and make sure that the food reaches 70°C for two minutes in different parts of the food. Temperature can be checked using a food probe.

How to use a food probe

Food probes are used to measure the temperature of food. There are many different types of probe; some can be linked to a computer to monitor temperature changes.

Insert the probe to a depth of 2 cm into the food. Wait for the temperature display to settle then record the reading. Each time the probe is used, wipe it with a bacterial food wipe. This will reduce the risk of cross-contamination of bacteria from one food to another. Do not push the food probe into frozen food as the probe might snap.

In the food industry, sensors monitor temperature changes in freezers, refrigerators, chill cabinets, ovens, cooling racks and storage facilities.

The Law and temperature control

The Food Safety (Temperature Control) Regulations 1995 require that perishable food should be kept at 8°C and below, and hot food should be kept at 63°C and above.

The microwave cooker

Microwaves heat up food by making the water molecules in the food vibrate, and this generates heat. Foods may not heat evenly when they are cooked in a microwave cooker. Food often needs to be stirred during cooking, to even out the temperature. Hot and cold spots are found in the food. A standing time is sometimes needed after cooking to allow the temperature in the food to even out. If food is not thoroughly cooked it may be unsafe to eat.

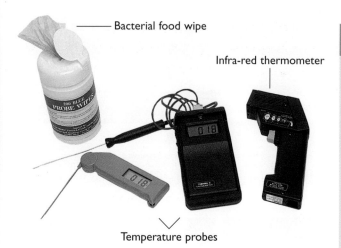

Bacterial food wipe

Infra-red thermometer

Temperature probes

Tools and equipment used to measure temperature

Questions

1 Make a list of the stages in making a food product that need temperature controls. Explain why these controls are important.

2 Explain how to use a food probe. How is a food probe useful when working with food? Why is it important to wipe the probe after inserting it into food?

3 Why is it important to make sure food is thoroughly cooked in a microwave cooker?

Planning and making

When making any food product, careful planning is needed to make sure that it is made in the correct way, that it comes up to a similar standard each time and that it is safe to eat. Plans may take the form of steps in a recipe, or flow diagrams. A flow diagram is a graphic way of showing a system.

Drawing flow diagrams

This is how you change the steps in a recipe to a detailed flow diagram. The flow diagram can show safety and quality checks. This is the recipe:

Baked potatoes filled with tuna and corn

4 baking potatoes, 2 tablespoons of soft cheese, 2 tablespoons sweetcorn, 100 g can tuna fish (drained)

Method

1   Wash the potatoes, make a cross in each one with a knife.

2   Either put on a baking tray and bake for 1 hour at 190°C or Gas Mark 5, or cook one potato at a time in a microwave oven on full power for about 5 minutes.

3   Beat the soft cheese and add the sweetcorn and tuna fish.

4   Check that the potatoes are cooked – insert a skewer to see if they are soft.

5   Cut open the potatoes and spoon the filling into each one.

6   Serve hot.

Flow diagram A shows the process for making the baked potato. Flow diagram B shows detail of Safety and Quality checks when making the baked potatoes. Each stage can then be checked for safety and quality as you make the product.

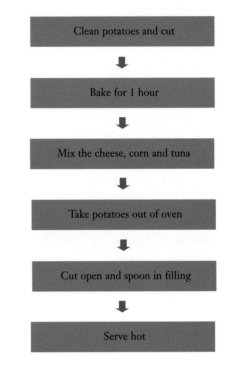

Flow diagram A – making a baked potato

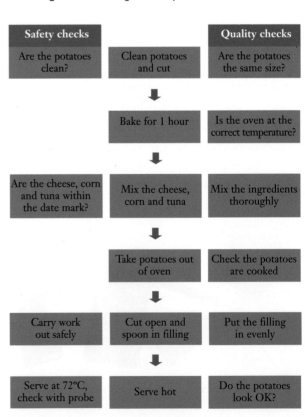

Flow diagram B – safety and quality checks

Symbols for a flow diagram

Some people like to use these symbols when drawing flow diagrams:

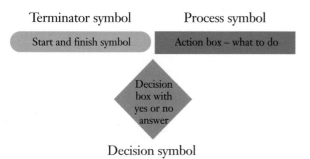

Flowcharts – terminator, process and decision symbols

The flow diagram for the baked potato could look like this – note that it is incomplete.

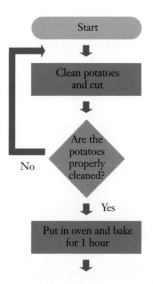

Flow diagram C – the flow diagram for baking a potato, using the alternative symbols

To do

1 Explain why safety and quality checks are important when you are making a food product.

2 Draw up a flow diagram to show how you would make an egg sandwich. Add the safety and quality checks for each stage.

3 Complete flow diagram C for the baked potato using the flow diagram symbols.

Planning in the food industry

The food industry has to be sure that its food products are safe to eat and meet quality standards. This chart shows the process for making scones and the safety and quality checks made by the scone manufacturer. The factory makes 25,000 scones an hour, so careful planning is essential before manufacturing food products on such a large scale. (More details of this work are on pages 26–28 in the Teacher's Resource Pack.)

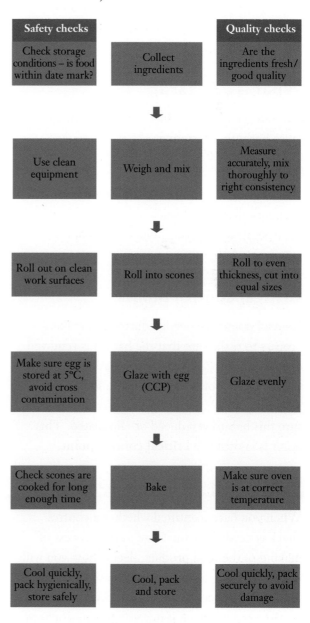

Making scones and the safety and quality checks

49

Hazard analysis

The food industry has to be very careful when preparing food products to make sure that they are safe to eat.

Hazard Analysis and Critical Control Point (HACCP)

This is a system used by food businesses to identify specific hazards and risks associated with food production and to describe ways to control these hazards.

What is a hazard?

A hazard in a food product is anything that can cause harm to a customer.

A hazard may be:

- biological, such as food poisoning bacteria
- chemical, such as bleach
- physical, such as glass, metal and other unwanted objects.

Critical control points

Control points are needed during the making process to make sure that the hazard is removed or reduced to a safe level. If the hazard is a high risk, in other words likely to cause food poisoning, then a control point is critical to make sure this hazard is reduced or eliminated. This point is known as a **critical control point.**

Tests to check on the process

When you have identified whether a control check is needed for the stage in the process of making of the food product, decide how you will test to see how the process can be checked. You may need to check by looking at the date-mark on the product to see if it is safe to eat, or check the temperature using a temperature probe.

How to draw up a HACCP system

1 Draw a flow diagram to show the making process for the food product.

2 Show any hazards for each step.

3 What control would you use for each stage?

4 Check if this is a critical control point.

5 Describe how you would test that the hazard had been checked.

This flow diagram shows the process for making a hot bagel with cream cheese to take away and eat from a shop.

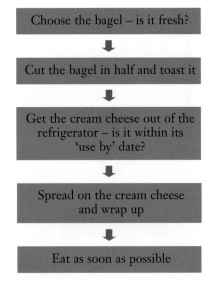

Choose the bagel – is it fresh?

⬇

Cut the bagel in half and toast it

⬇

Get the cream cheese out of the refrigerator – is it within its 'use by' date?

⬇

Spread on the cream cheese and wrap up

⬇

Eat as soon as possible

Flow diagram to show the process for making a hot bagel

A hot bagel with cream cheese

Identifying hazards

You can write a more detailed chart to identify any hazards showing the control steps to check these hazards and the tests you would use. The chart below is based on the information for the flow diagram for making the hot bagel with cream cheese. Extra headings have been added to help make a product which is safe to eat. These headings include 'Process' (similar to the flow diagram), 'Hazards', 'Control steps', 'Is it a critical control point?', 'Tests to check on the process'.

Process	Hazards	Control steps	Is it a critical control point?	Tests to check on the process
Choose the bagel	Could be old and mouldy	Is it fresh and clean?	No	Look at it and check the date-mark
Cut the bagel in half and toast	None	Make sure it is cut evenly and toasted until golden	No	Look at it
Get the cream cheese out of the refrigerator	Bacteria may be in the cream cheese	Is it within the 'use by' date? Is the refrigerator operating at 5°C or below?	Yes – the cream cheese can contain food poisoning bacteria	Check the date, use a temperature probe
Spread on the cream cheese and wrap up	Possibly if the cream cheese is left out	Work quickly and put the cheese back in the refrigerator	No	Look at it
Eat as soon as possible	Bacteria multiply in time	Make sure the bagel is eaten within one hour of purchase	Yes – if the bagel is left in a warm place and not eaten	Time: eat the bagel within two hours of preparation

Hazard analysis system for a hot bagel with cream cheese

To do

1 Draw a flow diagram for the following food products to show how they are made.

a a ham salad
b an omelette
c fairy cakes
d chicken soup

Alternatively, you could choose your own product.

2 For *one* of the products draw up a Hazard Analysis system. Use the headings shown in the chart above. Identify the possible hazards and add them to the chart. Include any critical control points which may be needed. Test the stages by looking at the quality of food, measuring the temperature, controlling the time and reading the date-marks on food products.

Modifying a food product

There are many reasons why you may want to adapt the ingredients and method of making a food product. Here are three examples.

Change the nutritional value – lowering the fat or sugar; increasing the fibre.

Alter the taste – making a dish more spicy or less salty.

Change the ingredients to meet special needs – taking the meat out of a pasta dish to make it suitable for vegetarians.

Why do food producers modify their food products?

People are told to eat less fat, sugar and salt and more fibre. Food producers modify their products to meet these nutritional demands, so you can buy low-fat yogurt, baked beans with reduced salt, sugar-free drinks and high-fibre bread.

People want to avoid animal fat, so food producers are using margarines that are suitable for vegetarians and creating food products that are suitable for vegetarians.

Sometimes ingredients are not available at the agreed price. If there is a poor apple harvest, the price of apples will go up and so apple pies may become more expensive and food producers may choose to make other kinds of fruit pies.

The taste and appearance of the product may need changing – if people have said that a product is too salty or too spicy, or it doesn't look attractive, the food producers need to modify the amount of salt or spices, add more colourful ingredients to the recipe or change the process.

Sometimes products just go out of fashion – sales of traditional products such as faggots are dropping, but veggie burgers are becoming more popular.

To do

Explain how you would modify the recipe for egg and bacon pasta to:

a lower the fat content

b increase the amount of fibre

c make it suitable for vegetarians.

First make the original recipe and keep a sample for tasting. Test out your modified recipe. Taste it carefully – you may have made a dish that does not taste as good as the original, so more modifications may be needed. Compare your modified recipe with the original recipe. How have your changes affected the appearance, flavour and appeal of the product?

Egg and bacon pasta

(Serves 2)

Ingredients
2 large eggs, 200 g dried pasta, 150 g streaky bacon, 50 g butter, 1 tablespoon oil 150 g grated cheese, black pepper.

Method
1 Boil the eggs for 10 minutes, cool then remove the shells and cut egg into slices.

2 Boil the pasta according to packet instructions then drain and toss in butter.

3 Chop up the bacon and fry in the oil until crisp.

4 Add the bacon, cheese and black pepper to the paste and serve topped with egg.

Labels on photo:
- Reduced sodium
- Reduced fat
- Meat free
- High fibre
- LO SALT (REDUCED SODIUM SALT ALTERNATIVE)
- Sugar free
- Fat free
- Low fat

These products have been modified in different ways

INGREDIENTS

CHICKEN · BROCCOLI · TOMATO · CHICKEN BOUILLON (WITH SOYA LECITHIN) · SINGLE CREAM · ONION · TOMATO PUREE · REDUCED FAT CHEDDAR CHEESE · MODIFIED STARCH · SALT · VEGETABLE OIL · LOW FAT MARGARINE (CONTAINS EMULSIFIER E471, STABILISER E401, PRESERVATIVE E202, COLOUR E160(a)) · WHEATFLOUR · GELLING AGENT · GELATINE · SUGAR · VEGETARIAN CHEESE FLAVOUR · VEGETABLE BOUILLON · GARLIC · PEPPER · MUSTARD.
MINIMUM 22% CHICKEN

St Michael

REDUCED FAT
Lite

CHICKEN, BROCCOLI & TOMATO

Tender pieces of boneless chicken with fresh broccoli in tomato sauce and cheese sauce topping

100% BREAST MEAT

LESS THAN **250 CALS** PER PACK

READY TO COOK — 255g ℮ 9 oz — DISPLAY UNTIL — USE BY — PRICE
KEEP REFRIGERATED 0°C to 5°C

≈ MICROWAVE OR CONVENTIONAL OVEN

The fat content in this product has been reduced

How do you modify your food designs?

Check if your design meets the brief – if a healthy product is needed, does your product meet these requirements?

Taste your product – do you need to change the ingredients to make it taste better, or alter the way it is made?

Check the method – do you need to change the process for better results?

To do

Collect labels of food products that have been modified. Look out for labels that make claims for changes such as 'new improved recipe' or 'lower in fat'. In each case, explain why you think the changes might have been made.

Questions

1 Give *three* reasons why:

a food producers modify their food products; in each case give an example of a food product

b you may need to adapt your food products. Give an example.

2 The label above for Chicken, broccoli and tomato has been adapted so that the product can meet the requirements of Reduced fat and Lite symbols. The Reduced fat symbol indicates that the fat content in the product is at least 25 per cent lower than in the regular product or similar ingredients. The Lite symbol indicates that the total energy content is at least 25 per cent lower than the regular product or similar ingredients. Suggest ways that you think this product could be adapted to meet these requirements by changing the type of ingredients used.

Quality

We expect food products to be of a 'good quality', but what does 'quality' mean for food producers? Think of the words you would use to describe a good quality sandwich – fresh, tasty, attractive, evenly filled. The food manufacturer has to make the sandwiches to this same quality all the time, so the company sets up a quality assurance procedure for the sandwich production. To do this, a flow diagram is drawn to show the sandwich making process, and quality checks are made at each stage in the process.

During food manufacture, the following quality checks can be made.

- Checking the quality of the ingredients for freshness, colour, size, cleanliness.
- Checking that raw ingredients, such as salads, are thoroughly cleaned.
- Weighing and measuring the ingredients and the final product, using a computer.
- Making sure that the mixing time is correct.
- Checking oven temperatures.
- Checking that the final product looks and tastes as expected.
- Checking that the product is made safely and hygienically.

To do

Choose a range of products such as biscuits, tomato sauces, bread and sandwiches. Discuss the words that describe the quality of each of these products. Keep a record of these quality descriptors – you can store the information on a computer **database** in a Quality word bank and use the descriptors for your food design.

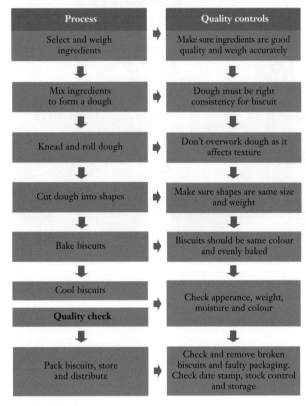

Process	Quality controls
Select and weigh ingredients	Make sure ingredients are good quality and weigh accurately
Mix ingredients to form a dough	Dough must be right consistency for biscuit
Knead and roll dough	Don't overwork dough as it affects texture
Cut dough into shapes	Make sure shapes are same size and weight
Bake biscuits	Biscuits should be same colour and evenly baked
Cool biscuits	Check apperance, weight, moisture and colour
Quality check	
Pack biscuits, store and distribute	Check and remove broken biscuits and faulty packaging. Check date stamp, stock control and storage

The quality checks made during the production of a biscuit

Word bank: quality

buttery, crisp, evenly baked, golden colour, regular shape

The word bank can also be shown on a star profile.

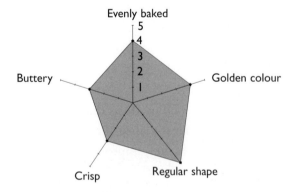

A star profile of biscuit quality

When making food products you can use these quality descriptors to check on the quality standards of your product.

What is the difference between quality assurance and quality control?

Quality assurance systems rely heavily on the expertise of food managers in identifying in advance where problems are likely to occur and setting up formal control systems to stop them happening. Quality assurance systems are replacing quality control as a concept. If quality controls are used on their own, faults are only identified after the product has been made, and then it must be either reworked or wasted.

Institute of Food Science and Technology

Case study

PRET À MANGER has approximately fifty cafés around the country. Leaflets in the cafés give details on the range and quality of food they sell and also explain their mission statement.

To do

Imagine that you have your own food company which sells food to the public. What range of products would you sell? What would your mission statement be for your company? Explain your quality requirements for two of your products. You could write a short statement like the one for PRET À MANGER carrot juice. Design and make a leaflet to show your ideas.

Questions

1 What is the difference between quality assurance and quality control?

2 List the quality statements that PRET À MANGER makes about its products on its leaflet. Explain how one of these quality statements could be useful when buying one of the products from a supplier.

Tasting and testing (1)

Food is made to be eaten, so tasting is essential if you are to judge the success of a food product. You can taste food products yourself, or get the help of others who become your tasting panel. When you are tasting food to get results to help with your design work, this is known as sensory analysis.

Tips on tasting food products

- Always check that everyone is able to taste the range of products. Ask if they have any food allergies or have any other reasons such as special dietary needs which prevent them from tasting certain foods.
- Taste food hygienically. Wash your hands before a tasting session, and make sure the tasting spoons and dishes are clean.
- If people are unwell, don't let them taste the food – they could spread infection to others.
- Provide tasting spoons, plastic cups and a place to dispose of waste food.
- Ask people not to talk as they taste food – one person can pass information on to another.
- Make sure the tasting is a fair test. Serve all food samples in the same way, on similar plates and dishes and at the same temperature.
- Label foods with random numbers or letters such as XAY so that people cannot identify the samples easily.
- Only taste up to six samples at a time – your taste buds can get tired of tasting!
- Clean your mouth with a large sip of water in between tasting food samples.
- Complete your tasting charts as you go along – you can easily forget how a food tastes.

Food producers organize food tasting

Using a tasting booth

A tasting booth is used for people to taste food samples quietly on their own. You can make a tasting booth using a piece of stiff card, or pieces of wood. Some schools have converted a small cupboard into a tasting booth, with coloured lights and a computer to record results.

Did you know?

The food industry trains people to work on tasting panels. Expert panellists have their taste buds tested! They have to be tested to see if they can tell the difference between sweet, sour, bitter and salty tastes and learn how to describe the characteristics of flavour and odour of foods. If people are unwell or have a cold, they cannot take part in tasting panels as their senses are not working fully and they may not be able to distinguish between different tastes. In the sensory appraisal booths in Sainsbury's, the lights change colour according to the food to be tested. If canned peaches are to be tested for flavour, a red light will hide the orange colour of the peaches, so that panellists judge the peaches on flavour not colour.

Taste

Different areas of the tongue respond to different tastes – sweetness is tasted near the tip, bitterness near the back, salt along the sides and acid down the middle.

Tasting charts

When you are tasting food products, there are many ways to get results. You can:

- find out which product people like the best
- identify one characteristic – for example, saltiness – and sort the products into order
- ask people to tell the difference between samples
- get detailed information on appearance, odour, flavour and texture (see chart below).

This chart shows detailed tasting notes for three samples of soup. The results can be used to help improve the recipe of the final product.

Star profile

If you are designing a product with a variety of tastes and flavours, you can draw a star profile to show what you would like it to taste like. Make the product and taste against the criteria.

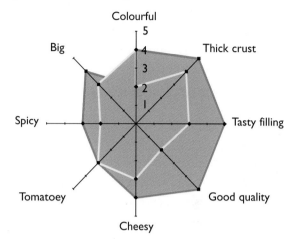

The star profile for a pizza

For more information on Tasting, see page 30–35 in the Teacher's Resource Pack.

Sample	XAY	DMN	PRT
Appearance	golden soup with chunks	yellowy soup with slivers	yellowy, brown, slightly greasy
Odour	fragrant and vegetably	carrot **aroma**	spicy
Flavour	too salty	mellow and vegetable flavour	good rounded flavour
Texture	thin and lumpy	creamy	creamy
Do you like it?	3/5 OK	5/5 excellent	4/5 quite nice
Order of liking	3	1	2

Tasting notes for three samples of soup

To do

See if you can tell the difference between sweet, sour, bitter and salty tastes. Make up some mixtures of liquids for each of these tastes. Sugar with water is sweet, lemon juice with water is sour, instant coffee mixed with water is bitter and salt with water is salty. Put each of the liquids into a tasting pot, and include a sample of plain water. Taste the five samples and decide which taste is which.

Questions

1 Why is it important to taste food before it is served or sold?

2 What is the purpose in using a tasting booth for food tasting?

3 Evaluate the star profile for a pizza. What changes need to be made so that the pizza meets the original design criteria?

Tasting and testing (2)

You need to develop your skills in tasting food. The experiments in tasting below will help to develop your knowledge about flavours and textures of food products. Everyone tastes food differently, so there is no right answer to any tasting session.

Experiment 1 – Jelly bean tasting

The colour of food may give you clues about the flavours you expect to taste. You may think that a red coloured drink will taste of fruit such as strawberry or raspberry. If you do not look at the food, then you are just using your tasting buds and sense of smell to get results. Carry out a **blind tasting** to test your tasting skills – this means you do not look at the food you are eating. You can try to taste the flavour of jelly beans for this experiment or, if you prefer, try to tell the difference between cheeses, milks or flavoured drinks.

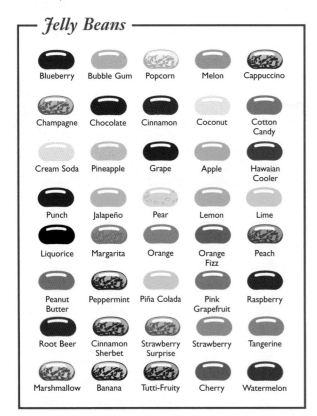

Jelly Beans

Blueberry	Bubble Gum	Popcorn	Melon	Cappuccino
Champagne	Chocolate	Cinnamon	Coconut	Cotton Candy
Cream Soda	Pineapple	Grape	Apple	Hawaian Cooler
Punch	Jalapeño	Pear	Lemon	Lime
Liquorice	Margarita	Orange	Orange Fizz	Peach
Peanut Butter	Peppermint	Piña Colada	Pink Grapefruit	Raspberry
Root Beer	Cinnamon Sherbet	Strawberry Surprise	Strawberry	Tangerine
Marshmallow	Banana	Tutti-Fruity	Cherry	Watermelon

Varieties of jelly beans

Sample	Flavour	Colour	Tasting words to describe the bean

Tasting chart for jelly beans

To do

You need

- a selection of flavoured jelly beans
- a glass of water to clear the palate
- tasting chart

Work in a group. One member of the group selects and keeps a record of the flavours of jelly beans used in the tasting session. Each member of the tasting panel follows these steps.

- Taste each of the beans and identify the flavours and colours without looking at the beans – this is the blind tasting.
- Write down some words to describe the flavours.
- Sip some water and taste another bean.
- Compare the tasting results with the flavours and colours of the beans.
- Which flavours were easy to identify? Which ones were more difficult?
- Discuss why some of the flavours were hard to identify.

Questions

1 Make a list of all the words which you used to describe the flavour of the jelly beans during this tasting. These words are called sensory descriptors and you can keep them as a tasting word bank.

2 Suggest some flavours with their names that could be added to a jelly bean range. Give reasons for your choices.

Experiment 2 – Apple tasting

Sainsbury's, the supermarket chain, has designed a chart to show five different levels of sweetness for a range of apples. This information is displayed in its supermarkets to help shoppers choose the variety of apple they prefer.

An apple divider

Levels of sweetness	Apple variety
1 sharp	Cooking apples, Granny Smith
2 fairly sharp	Braeburn, McIntosh
3 sharp and sweet	Cox, Russets
4 fairly sweet	Golden Delicious, Red dessert apples
5 sweet	Royal Gala, Fuji

Levels of sweetness of apples

This apple divider is used to divide the apple into equal sized portions for tasting which helps in this classroom activity.

Experiment 3 – Cheese tasting

When some people buy cheese, they like to know how strong it is. Sainsbury's has designed a strength guide to buying cheese.

1 = mild, 2 = mellow, 3 = medium, 4 = strong, 5 = very strong

To do

1 Carry out an apple tasting with several different varieties of apples. Sort the apples into levels of sweetness and compare your results with those on the chart.

2 As you taste each apple, write down words to describe the flavour and texture. You can record your results on a star profile and then compare the tastes of the different apples.

New Strength Guide to Buying Cheese

1 Mild	**2** Mellow	**3** Medium
4 Strong	**5** Very Strong	

Cheese strength guide

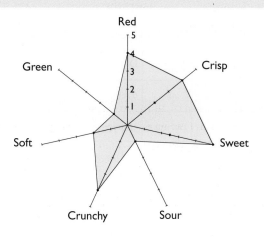

Star profile for apples

To do

Buy a range of cheeses which show the strength guide and cut them into small pieces. Carry out a blind tasting. Try to sort the cheeses into order of strength. Write your own sensory descriptors for each cheese. Draw a star profile to show the flavour of each cheese.

Cooking and serving instructions

A food label may show cooking and serving instructions, to tell people how to prepare the food product for eating. The food producers have tested the instructions for the dishes many times to make sure that they are cooked thoroughly, that the food reaches the right temperature (above 70°C for at least two minutes) and that the product is served in the best condition. (See page 51 in the Teacher's Resource Pack for more information.) Here is a collection of cooking instructions from food labels.

Tuscan bean soup

**KEEP WELL
REFRIGERATED
EAT WITHIN 24 HOURS
OF OPENING**

This soup is best served hot.

CONVENTIONAL HEATING

Shake well, pour soup into saucepan, heat gently, stirring occasionally. Do not boil. Season to taste.

TO MICROWAVE

800 watt Microwave ovens vary in performance. The following recommendation is a guide only. Shake well. Open top of pack completely. Place in microwave and heat on high for 5 minutes.

**STIR SOUP HALFWAY THROUGH
COOKING TIME. CARTON WILL BE
HOT – HANDLE WITH CARE.**

Allow to stand for 2 minutes before serving. Check that soup is hot before serving.

**DO NOT REHEAT
SUITABLE FOR HOME FREEZING**

For best results heat from frozen at low temperature and stir well.

SERVING SUGGESTION

Serve with sautée slices of cabbage or slivers of red onion and ciabatta bread.

Crusty bread with Marmite and butter

The timings given below are a guide only as variations between differing appliances can occur.

TO OVEN BAKE: Remove all packaging, including film bag. Place on a baking tray and heat in a pre-heated oven at 200°C/400°F/Gas Mark 6 for 12–14 minutes until crisp and golden.

To heat in a fan assisted or combination oven adjust the heating time referring to manufacturer's instructions.

Ensure the food is piping hot throughout before serving.

DO NOT REHEAT

Chicken tikka masala

Conventional oven

Remove sleeve and pierce film lid. Place on a baking tray in a preheated oven 180°C/Gas Mark 4 for 20 minutes.

From frozen

Remove sleeve and pierce film lid. Place on a baking tray in a preheated oven 190°C/Gas Mark 5 for 40 minutes.

Microwave

Remove sleeve and pierce film lid. Place on a non-metallic plate and microwave on full power for:

	Heating category		Wattage	
	B	D	650	750
From chilled	7 mins	6 mins	7 mins	6 mins
From frozen	11.5 mins	9.5 mins	11.5 mins	9.5 mins

Stir well before serving. Check that the product is piping hot before serving. Do not reheat.

Writing your own cooking and serving instructions

You can write your own cooking and serving instructions for a food product, but you will need to carry out temperature and quality tests first.

To do

If you make this recipe for Chilli con carne at school, you will need to reheat it at home. Instructions for reheating have been given on the recipe. Test them out to see if the product reaches at least 70°C for at least two minutes. You will need a temperature probe for accurate measurement. Insert the probe to a depth of 2 cm in the centre and edges of the dish. Work in groups and make several portions for testing.

Steps

1 Make the recipe (or adapt it to suit your tastes), and cool it.

2 Choose different ways to reheat the chill con carne:

- in an oven
- in a microwave cooker
- by steaming over boiling water.

3 Test how long it takes to reach 70°C and above for two minutes.

4 Write up your results.

5 Write the information as it would be shown on a food label. The instructions for Spaghetti Bolognaise on page 63 may give you a few tips. Describe how you would serve the Chilli con carne.

To do

Design your own cooking instructions for a food product that needs reheating. Use information on these pages to give you guidelines.

Chilli Con Carne

1 INGREDIENTS (serves two people)

- 225g lean minced beef
- 75g onion – finely chopped
- clove of garlic – crushed (optional)
- 2 tablespoons tomato purée
- salt and pepper
- 1 teaspoon hot chilli sauce (alter according to taste)
- 1 small can red kidney beans (approx. 220g)

2 METHOD

- Fry the minced beef, onion and garlic (if used) together in a saucepan for 4–5 minutes until the meat is browned. Drain off any excess fat.
- Stir in the tomato purée, salt, pepper, chilli sauce and kidney beans with their juice.
- Cover the pan with a lid and cook gently for 10 minutes until the mixture is thick. Stir occasionally

3 TAKE HOME TIPS

Cover and reheat for 20 minutes 200°C/ Gas Mark 6. **OR** Microwave 4–5 minutes, turning half way. Serve with boiled rice and salad.

Recipe for Chilli con carne

Questions

1 The Tuscan bean soup and the Chicken tikka masala can be reheated in the microwave cooker, but the Crusty bread with Marmite and butter has to be oven-baked. Why? Give reasons.

2 Why does the food cooked in the microwave cooker have to be stirred before serving?

3 How would you check that the food was 'piping hot'?

Portion control

When food is served at meal-times or sold as ready meals, you usually need to know the size of a portion.

What is a portion?

A portion for one is the amount of food that satisfies the needs of one person, but the weight and size of a portion of cake, for example, can vary depending on how much you like to eat.

The book, *Food Portion Sizes*, published by the Ministry of Agriculture, Fisheries and Food (MAFF), provides information on typical weights and portion sizes of foods eaten in Britain. The information in the book has been collected by carefully weighing items of food, and also using details from food producers. This book is useful if you want to:

- work out how much of each food ingredient to use in a meal
- find the weight of an ingredient such as an apple or carrot
- calculate the nutritional value of a meal based on the average weight of the ingredients.

Packing food by weight

Most food products have the weight, size or number listed on the packet. Only some food products have to be packed in specific weights. Examples include chocolate bars, bags of flour and cereals. The size and portions of other food products such as ready meals, are chosen by the food manufacturer, so the portions can vary in size.

To do

Guess the weight for a portion of each of the foods listed below. You could decide how much you would eat and enter these results. The answers are on page 96, under the Index.

a a medium portion of chips
b a small packet of crisps
c a scoop of ice-cream
d a portion of lasagne for one
e pizza, 18 cm in diameter
f a crusty bread roll.

Chips

Bag of crisps

Ice-cream

Lasagne for one

Crusty bread roll

Pizza, 18 cm diameter

How much do these portions of food weigh?

Spaghetti Bolognaise label

1 In the book, *Food Portion Sizes*, the researchers have compared the weight of ready-made Spaghetti Bolognaise with the home-made and restaurant versions. Here are the results.

Type of Spaghetti Bolognaise meal	Weight
frozen ready meal for one: pasta 100 g, sauce 220 g	320 g
average home-made portion	470 g
restaurant portion: pasta 230 g, sauce 170 g	400 g

a Comment on these results. Why do you think the portion sizes vary?

b What is the portion size for Spaghetti Bolognaise on the label shown?

2 Collect a range of food labels which show portion sizes. Try to collect labels for similar products such as lasagne or beefburgers. Compare the results by listing the products, their weight and cost.

The cost of food products

We need to know how much food costs, as we usually have a limit on the amount of money we can spend on shopping and eating out. Food producers also need to work out the costs of making a food product before they start production, if they are to run a profitable business.

Costing a recipe

To work out the cost of a recipe, list the ingredients and the quantity used. Keep a record of how much the ingredients cost to buy. You could store the information on a computer database.

Some ingredients such as flour, sugar and butter are sold prepacked, and you cannot buy the exact quantity you need. Sugar is sold in one kilogram bags, so you need to know the cost of the kilo bag, the quantity of sugar you use, and then you can work out the cost of sugar used in the recipe. This can be done using a calculator or with a computer spreadsheet.

For more information see pages 36–37 in the Teacher's Resource Pack.

Using a computer spreadsheet

Designing within cost limits

Food businesses have to set limits on the costs of making food products. School lunches, Meals on Wheels, hospital and airline meals all have to be prepared within budget limits. These budgets include the cost of ingredients, and also the labour costs to make the meals. Food designers have to change and modify recipes (formulations) to meet budget limits.

To do

1 Create the exact recipe for a pizza which must cost less than £1.30, using the pizza base and costings shown on the chart on page 65.

Topping suggestions – 75 g tomatoes, 50–75g grated cheese plus any extras of your choice. The list of ingredients shows the cost per 100g. Add you own ideas. Show how you have costed out the recipe. You may need to test out your ideas to check the weights you have suggested to see if they work.

Create a pizza

Ingredients	Cost per item or 100 g
pizza base (ready made)	52p each
tomatoes, chopped and canned	8p per 100 g
fresh tomatoes	20p per 100 g
mild Cheddar	36p per 100 g
mature Cheddar	61p per 100 g
Farmhouse Cheddar	76p per 100 g
grated Cheddar cheese	56p per 100 g
grated pizza cheese	66p per 100 g
salami	130p per 100 g
ham	95p per 100 g
olives	60p per 100 g

List of ingredients showing cost per 100 g

2 The pizza recipe below is too expensive. Show the changes you would make in the ingredients and the quantities used to meet the design limits of £1.30.

pizza base	52p
tomatoes 75 g	6p
grated pizza cheese 75 g	50p
olives 10 g	6p
salami 20 g	26p
total cost	**£1.40**

Costing food products on a large scale

The food industry keeps strict control on the costs of raw materials (ingredients) used in food manufacture. If there is a poor harvest or other disaster, the cost of raw materials may rise, and then substitutes will need to be found. For example, a soup manufacturer which specialized in carrot and coriander soup found that the carrot crop failed in one country, so the buyers had to find carrots from another part of the world, which led to an increase in the cost of making the soup.

The cost of making a food product on a large scale

Food businesses must include the costs of their overheads, which can include costs such as labour, rent of factory, storage of ingredients, equipment and distribution of the product. A large food business has different costs for overheads than a small business. Large food producers can purchase their raw materials more cheaply than smaller businesses, since they can buy in bulk, in large quantities from their suppliers.

How can you compare the costs of home-made with large-scale costs?

Here is an idea from a food designer, to show how she estimates the selling price of a product.

Formula for working out the selling price

1 Work out the costs of supermarket ingredients to make the product.

2 Take off 30 per cent from that cost – this result is an estimate of the cost of the ingredients to a large food business.

3 What about overheads? Multiply the lower cost of ingredients by three.

Large-scale costing formula

Selling price = (cost of ingredients – 30% of this cost) x 3

Questions

1 If food products are made on a large scale in a factory, what are the extra costs that have to be added on to the costs of the food ingredients, to work out the selling price?

2 If it costs £1 to make a cake using ingredients bought from a supermarket, estimate how much the selling price of the cake might be, using the formula shown above.

Preserving foods

Food is preserved to help it keep longer. For thousands of years people have used different ways to preserve food, and many traditional methods are still used today.

Method	Examples	How it works
salting	salted fish such as cod, olives, salami	The salt kills micro-organisms and stops their growth.
pickling	vegetables in vinegar, such as onions and turnips	The acid in the vinegar prevents the growth of micro-organisms.
smoking	smoked fish and cheese	Chemicals in the smoke prevent the growth of micro-organisms.
jamming	fruit jams such as blackcurrant and strawberry	Sugar in the jam prevents the growth of micro-organisms.
drying	dried peas, potatoes, rice	Micro-organisms cannot grow without moisture.
Low temperatures freezing	frozen peas, ice-cream, fish fingers	Freezing at −18°C stops the micro-organisms from multiplying and growing.
chilling	chilled ready meals	Growth of micro-organisms in food chilled at or below 8°C is slowed down.
High temperatures **canning** and bottling	canned soups, beans, fruit	High temperatures kill or remove most micro-organisms.
UHT (Ultra Heat Treatment)	used for milk and juices	These products need to be packed and sealed in sterile conditions.
irradiation	seasonings such as pepper and spices	Micro-organisms are destroyed by passing energy waves through the product.
MAP (Modified Atmosphere Packaging)	packing food such as salads	Exchange of gases slows down growth of micro-organisms.

Chart to show ways of preserving food

Hot Pack™ self heating meals have been designed for people who want a hot meal without having to carry bulky cooking equipment and food ingredients. The Hot Pack™ comes with a cooked meal in a pouch with a tray, knife, fork, salt and pepper, serviette, heater sleeve and a sachet of water to use in the heater. The heater sleeve contains chemicals which, when mixed with water, react and produce heat. The food in the pouch will reach 80°C within 12–15 minutes depending on the outside temperature.

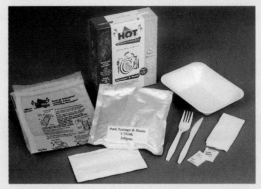

Hot Pack™ with pouch, tray, fork, knife, salt, pepper, serviette and heater sleeve

Home food dehydrator

Traditionally food is dried by leaving it for several days in the sun. An electric dehydrator can be used for drying food at home. Hot air rises through trays of food, and the trays are rotated gently to make sure the food is dried evenly. The dehydrator removes 95 per cent of the moisture content from the food and takes about eight hours. When the food has been dried it can be stored in jars or tins until it is needed.

For more information see pages 38–41 in the Teacher's Resource Pack.

Dehydrators for drying fruits

Additives which are preservatives

Preservatives in the form of **additives** are often added to food products to prevent, slow down or stop the growth of micro-organisms (bacteria, fungi, mould and yeast) which cause food decay and health hazards. These preservatives help to increase the shelf life of the product so that it will last longer.

> **Apple pie**
>
> **Ingredients:** Apples with preservative, ascorbic acid, citric acid, wheatflour, sugar, butter, starch, gelling agent: pectin

Apple pie label

Questions

1 Give *three* reasons why people preserve food.

2 Read the case study for Hot Pack™ meals. What groups of people would use this product in the UK? Give reasons for your answer.

3 Explain why additives are used as preservatives in many food products. What preservatives are used in the label for Apple pie? What are your views on the use of additives? Do you think they are needed or not? Give your reasons.

How long will food keep?

Shelf life

The shelf life of a food product is the length of time it will remain wholesome and safe to eat, if stored under the recommended conditions. Food can be stored at different temperatures.

Temperature of storage	Examples
Room temperature (ambient temperature, 20–25°C)	vegetables, fruit, bread, biscuits, flour, canned and bottled products
Chilled temperature (food at 8°C or below)	meat, poultry, milk, cheese, **cook-chill** products
Frozen (in a freezer at –18°C or below)	meat, poultry, fish, ice-cream, meals

Temperatures at which food can be stored

To do

Place the listed food products on a copy of the time line chart below to show how long they will stay safe and tasty to eat.

The time line shows very short time, short time, medium time and long time. Some examples have been completed.

Comment on the results. What methods of processing and storage give food:

a   the shortest shelf life
b   the longest shelf life?

Time line	Examples
very short time	fresh fish
short time	chilled ready meals
medium time	frozen chips
long time	canned orange juice

Time line chart

Fish – fresh fish, frozen fish, canned fish such as tuna and salmon, dried fish, fish made into ready meals such as fisherman's pie

Tomatoes – fresh tomato, canned tomatoes, tomato sauce

Milk – fresh, dried, UHT, sterilized, pasteurized

Orange juice – freshly squeezed, concentrate, UHT, canned, frozen

Custard – fresh, canned, dried, ambient stable

Potatoes – fresh, frozen as chips, dried, crisps, extruded snacks, chilled ready meals, frozen ready meals

Instant mashed potatoes

Frozen chips

Potato fritters

Potato waffles

Fresh potatoes

Potato snacks

Potato in a ready meal

Potato products

Shelf life date-marking

The shelf life of a food product is shown by the 'use by', 'best before' and 'best before end' date-mark on the food label. This date depends on whether the food has been stored according to instructions.

The quality of food changes during storage. Flavour, texture and appearance deteriorate with age, although some foods improve, such as Worcestershire sauce. Some foods become dangerous to eat if they are kept after the 'use by' date. Foods such as bread become stale.

Food design and shelf life

It is difficult to compare the shelf life of a food product in a supermarket with a school-made version because:

- food in supermarkets can be stored at very low temperatures to prolong shelf life
- commercial food products may use preservatives and anti-oxidants which are not easily available for school use
- processing such as canning, drying and freezing cannot easily be copied at school
- the gas inside some food packaging is exchanged to prevent deterioration – this is known as Modified Atmosphere Packaging (MAP) and cannot be imitated at school
- packaging can protect the product from damage or deterioration.

In addition, in school you cannot tell if food contains dangerous levels of pathogenic bacteria.

For safety, do not carry out tests to see how long it takes a food to deteriorate.

The food industry uses computer programs to carry out predictive **modelling** of bacterial growth and this can help to determine the shelf life of a product.

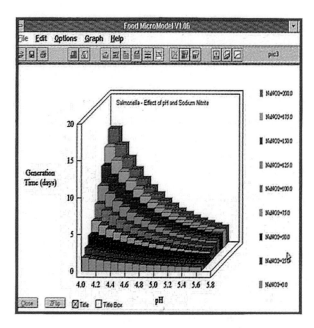

Food MicroModel to show modelling of bacterial growth

Tips on designing food for a longer shelf life

- Make sure that you use fresh ingredients for your food products.
- Prepare foods in clean and hygienic food areas.
- Cool cooked food within 90 minutes and store at a temperature below 5°C. Cover thoroughly and label with a date mark.
- Cakes and biscuits should be stored in an airtight tin in a cool place, so that moisture cannot soften the products.
- Fruits such as strawberries can be made into jams and jellies, or frozen to increase shelf life.

Questions

1 What is meant by the 'shelf life' of a food product?

2 Describe *four* ways in which food can be processed to increase shelf life.

3 Why does food made on a large scale usually have a longer shelf life than home-made food?

Food labels

Food labels give us lots of information about a food product. For most food products the label must include:

- the product name
- an ingredients list in descending order of weight
- the shelf life – the 'use by' or 'best before' date
- storage instructions
- the name and address – may be the manufacturer, packer or **EU** seller
- the origin
- instructions for use
- the weight of the product.

The big **e** beside the weight of a product means that the average quantity must be accurate.

Food companies can choose whether or not to provide nutrition information. If a nutrition claim is made on the label, then the label must show nutrition information.

The label may also show serving suggestions, a bar code, information such as whether the product is suitable for vegetarians, and if the packaging can be **recycled.**

Questions

Use the label for Carrot and Coriander soup to answer these questions.

1 Copy the chart below and complete it to show how the information is shown on the soup label.

	Information from soup label
Product name	
Company name	
Company logo	
Name and address	
Ingredients list in descending order of weight	
Shelf life – the 'use by' or 'best before' date	
Instructions for use	
Weight of the product	
Storage instructions	
Other useful information	

Chart on information for a soup

2 What are the three main ingredients in this recipe, and what are the functions of these ingredients (functions include flavour, colour, texture, thickening, thinning)?

3 How should this soup be served? Give exact details.

4 Why does the label state 'do not reheat'?

5 What is meant by an 'e' by the weight section?

USE BY

KEEP REFRIGERATED

U-7979
U-7979
7979 07915

EUROPAK

PURE-PAK™

OPEN OTHER SIDE

ALL NATURAL INGREDIENTS

NEW COVENT GARDEN SOUP CO

3. Pull out diagonally opposite corners

4. Repeat 3 to fully open pack

1. Tear open. Push right back

2. Turn carton round and repeat 1 on opposite side

NEW COVENT GARDEN SOUP CO

THE ART OF SOUP MAKING

FRESH

CARROT & CORIANDER

S O U P

The art of soup making is to combine top quality, fresh ingredients with a wholesome and subtly seasoned stock. We use the same natural ingredients you might expect to find in your own kitchen.

Carrot and Coriander is a refreshing combination of carrots and coriander enhanced by the addition of fresh dairy cream and a hint of nutmeg.

SUITABLE FOR VEGETARIANS

THERE ARE NO PRESERVATIVES, COLOURINGS OR OTHER ADDITIVES.

INGREDIENTS: Water, Carrots, Onions, Cream, Flour, Butter, Vegetable Stock, Salt, Garlic, Coriander, Nutmeg.

NUTRITIONAL INFORMATION	
	Average per 100 ml
ENERGY	208 kJ
	50 kcal
PROTEIN	0.9 g
CARBOHYDRATE	5.7 g
of which sugars	2.7 g
FAT	2.8 g
of which saturates	1.6 g
FIBRE	0.8 g
SODIUM	0.3 g

As our soup is only made from natural ingredients, nutritional values may vary.

© NCGSC '95

SERVING SUGGESTION

℮ 568 ml 1 pint serves 2-3

KEEP REFRIGERATED. EAT WITHIN 24 HRS OF OPENING.
This soup can be served hot or chilled.
CONVENTIONAL HEATING: Shake well, pour soup into saucepan, heat gently, stirring occasionally. Do not boil. Season to taste.
TO MICROWAVE: 800 watt. Microwave ovens vary in performance. The following recommendation is a guide only. Shake well. Open top of pack completely. Place in microwave and heat on high for 5 minutes.
STIR SOUP HALFWAY THROUGH COOKING TIME. CARTON WILL BE HOT – HANDLE WITH CARE.
Allow to stand for 2 minutes before serving. Check that soup is hot before serving.
DO NOT REHEAT
SUITABLE FOR HOME FREEZING: For best results, heat from frozen at low temperature and stir well.
SERVING SUGGESTION: Garnish with a swirl of yoghurt and fresh herbs.

5 016516 000033

The New Covent Garden Soup Company Ltd.
35 Hythe Road, London, NW10 6RS.

Carrot and Coriander soup

Further work

6 Estimate how many Calories are provided by a serving of this soup.

7 Which ingredients supply the following nutrients and fibre?

Nutrient	Ingredients which supply the nutrient
carbohydrate	
fat	
fibre	
sodium	

Packaging food products

Why do we need to package food?

- Packaging around food protects it from damage.
- It helps to keep food away from dirt and bacteria.
- The packaging can be attractive and provide information.
- Packaging helps with handling the product during transportation and storage.
- Packaging can help a product to keep longer (increases shelf life).
- Packaging reduces food waste by protecting it from damage.

Recycling waste packaging

The food industry often uses packaging which can be recycled. However, food must not come into direct contact with recycled packaging, as the food could become contaminated.

For more work on recycled packaging see pages 44–5 in the Teacher's Resource Pack.

 Pizza Hut is working to help the environment. You can too by disposing of this box carefully

THE TIDY BRITAIN GROUP

 Pizza Hut®

This box is 100% recyclable and **biodegradable**, having been made from renewable, sustainable pulp resources.

 RECYCLING

Pizza Hut package label

Material	Function	Uses
paper and board	strong and lightweight, but does not protect from damp; can be recycled	bags, boxes, cartons
plastic	flexible, strong, lightweight, can be printed, quite expensive to recycle	bottles, trays, wrapping materials
metal	strong and rigid, can be printed on, can be recycled	drink cans, trays, foil wrap
glass	easily recycled, strong, but can can break	bottles, jars

Chart to show materials used in packaging

Packaging your food product

The chart opposite shows useful words to describe the packaging for food products. Think about the type of packaging you will use, and the shape of the packaging. If the packaging is made out of paper or card, you could draw a net to show how the package will be constructed.

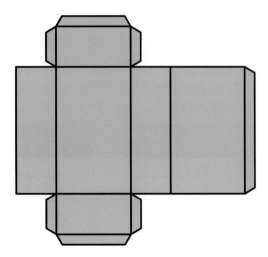

A net for packaging

Material for packaging	Words to describe the packaging
paper, board, plastic, metal glass	see-through, thick, thin, easy-to-open, inexpensive, rigid, soft, recyclable, stackable, waterproof, solid, colourful, protective, flexible, essential, luxury, used in the microwave, used in the oven, porous, easy to print on, strong, reusable, transparent, lightweight

Packaging word bank

To do

Choose *three* of the words that describe the packaging.

Describe a packaging that would match these words.

Think about words to describe the function of your packaging. You could create a Packaging word bank – brainstorm ideas in a group. For example, you may want your packaging to be colourful, rigid, able to be used in a microwave.

You could draw a star profile to show the results.

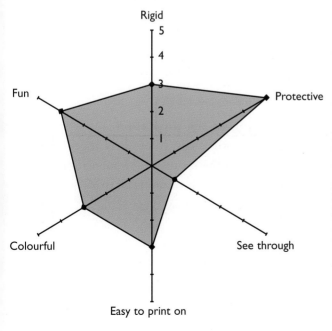

A star profile for packaging

If you want to design the label and the packaging, use a drawing package on the computer.

Information needed on food packaging

- food product with name
- company logo and address
- ingredients, weight, cost, nutrition content, shelf life
- instructions for use and storage instructions

Questions

1 List the functions of the packaging for each of the following food products: eggs in carton, pizza in box with polystyrene holder, cereal box with plastic lining, fizzy drink with ring pull can, still fruit drink in glass bottle with metal lid, ready meal in plastic dish inside a cardboard box.

Words to use: protects, attractive, carries advertising, helps with handling, keeps safe, provides nutrition information, increases shelf life.

Packaging for food products

2 For each food product in question 1, suggest what material is used for the packaging and say how it can be recycled.

3 What is meant by the following terms used on the Pizza Hut packaging?
a 100% recyclable
b biodegradable
c renewable, sustainable pulp resources

Making food in quantity

Large-scale simulation

You can explore the challenges of making food on a large scale by carrying out a **simulation** (mock-up) of the process of making the food product.

To do

Choose a food product that you can use in school in large quantities. The aim of the simulation is to make the products to the same quality standards each time, to have the same accuracy of finish and to find and solve problems as they arise. Examples of food products might be:

- biscuits for a school fair
- mince pies for a Christmas celebration
- pizzas or soup for a class lunch.

Biscuits, mince pies, pizza

You need to use accurate digital scales to check weights and a clean ruler to measure products.

Work in teams

- List the steps to make and cook the product.

- Decide which members of the team will carry out each step.

- List the quality checks you need for each step.

- Choose a team member to carry out the quality checks and reject products not meeting the standards.

- One member of the team can record problems and changes made.

Process	Quality checks
Choose ingredients	Are they within the date-mark?
Mix	Is the dough thoroughly mixed?
Roll out	Is the dough evenly rolled?
Cut	Are the biscuits cut to a similar size and shape?
Reroll spare biscuit dough	Is the spare dough rolled evenly?
Bake in oven	Are the biscuits baking to the same colour?
Cool	Are the biscuits cooled in hygienic conditions?
Pack	Are the biscuits packed in hygienic conditions?

Example: making biscuits on a large scale

Reporting on the simulation

Keep a record as you go of the changes made, and evaluate the results of the simulation. Weigh the amount of products that you rejected. Comment on these results.

Making the products in a factory

This chart shows the process of making biscuits on a large-scale in a factory.

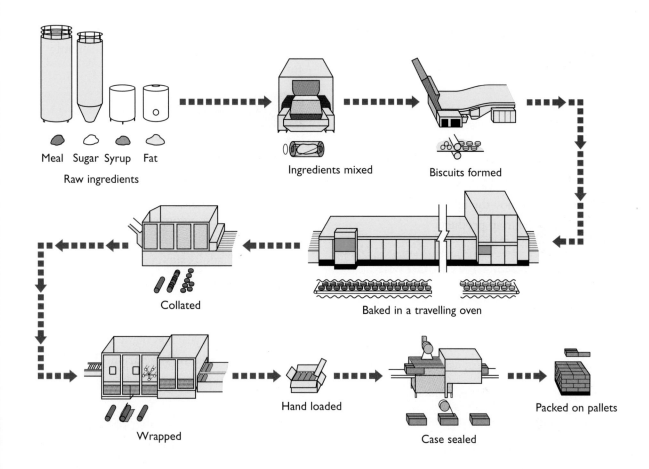

Making biscuits in McVitie's digestive biscuit factory

A factory would use computers to check standards throughout the process.

Large-scale mixers and ovens would also be used. This chart shows the production of McVities biscuits. You can see that a large travelling oven is used to cook the biscuits. The biscuits travel through the oven as they cook.

To do

Draw a flow diagram to show the process of making biscuits in the factory.

At each stage show the quality checks needed to make sure that quality standards are met.

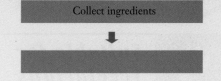

Foods for vegetarians (1)

In the UK nearly seven million people are vegetarian or have cut down on eating meat. Each year more and more people choose to eat vegetarian food. Why do people become vegetarians?

- People do not like the thought that animals are killed for food.
- Certain religious groups follow a vegetarian diet.
- People are concerned about the environment and feel that meat production is expensive.
- Some people think that a vegetarian diet is healthy.
- Many people enjoy the taste and the wide choice of vegetarian products.

Different types of vegetarian

A vegetarian eats no meat, poultry or fish and avoids products made from slaughtered animals, such as gelatine.

Lacto-ovo vegetarians – eat dairy products and eggs.

Lacto vegetarians – eat dairy products but not eggs.

Vegans – eat no animal products at all.

Demi-vegetarians – don't eat red meat, but do eat white meat or fish.

Vegetarian symbols used for food products

Symbols for vegetarian food

Food products are usually labelled with symbols or statements to show that they are suitable for vegetarians.

Did you know?

- The number of vegetarians in the UK has increased by 42 per cent between 1985 and 1995. (Realeat Polls)
- Vegetarianism is rising with 0.5 per cent of the population converting each year to become vegetarian. (The Vegetarian Society)
- Of 1000 adults surveyed, 40 per cent eat less red meat than they did five years ago. (Del Monte Healthy Lifestyle Report 1995)
- The 21st Century Report estimates that over the next ten years, as many as one person in five may become vegetarian. (Frozen Food Information Service)

This chart shows the number of vegetarians and people choosing to eat less meat. You will see that the results from the different surveys vary.

	Vegetarian	People eating less meat
Vegetarian Society	5%	12%
Meat and Livestock Commission	3%	9%
Daily Telegraph	7%	17%
BBC Watchdog	(not available)	23%
Independent	7%	(not available)

Trends in people becoming vegetarian or eating less meat

Know your ingredients

When you are designing food for vegetarians, you need to check that the ingredients do not contain animal products. The chart below shows some ingredients that need careful checking.

Ingredient	Changes for vegetarian choices
Gelatine (made from animal bones and skin)	Look at the labels for jellies, yogurt, sweets and ice-cream and choose agar-agar instead.
Animal fat	Look at the labels on biscuits, breads and desserts and use vegetable fat instead.
Cheeses	Some cheeses state 'suitable for vegetarians': these are not made with rennet taken from calves' stomachs.
E numbers	E120 is made from cochineal, and E542 from edible bone phosphate so these should be avoided by vegetarians.
Vitamin D	This may come from lanolin in sheeps' wool.
Worcester Sauce	Often made from anchovies.
Eggs	Some vegetarians prefer to eat free range eggs. Processed foods usually contain eggs from battery farms.

Source: Healthy eating for vegetarians, J. Sainsbury

Questions

1 What are the names of the different groups of vegetarians and what is the difference in their food choices?

2 Explain why the following food ingredients are not suitable for vegetarians.

a gelatine
b some E numbers
c certain types of cheese
d margarine which is not labelled 'made from vegetable oil'

3 Look at the following lists of ingredients.

Apple crumble

Ingredients
Apple, wheatflour, sugar, margarine, breadcrumbs, water, starch

Thickened yogurt

Ingredients
Yogurt, added ingredients – sugar, flavouring, gelatine

Strawberry flavour jelly

Ingredients
Glucose syrup, sugar solution, water, gelatine, citric acid, acidity regulator, cochineal, flavouring

How would you adapt each of these products to make them suitable for vegetarians?

Note: Cochineal is the red colouring which comes from the cochineal beetle.

Apple crumble

Yogurt

Strawberry jelly

4 Comment on why you think the figures in the vegetarian chart on page 76 vary.

Foods for vegetarians (2)

Meat replacements for vegetarians

These are some of the food ingredients which can be used in recipes as replacements for meat. These ingredients are good sources of protein and some provide dietary fibre, vitamins and minerals.

Soya mince

Red split lentils

Tofu

Butter beans

Quorn

Soya mince

Red kidney beans

A range of meat substitutes – beans

Beans and pulses

Beans and pulses include lentils, peas and beans such as kidney beans. Beans and pulses can be used for many recipes including pasta dishes, curries, dips, salads and burgers.

Beans and pulses are often sold dried and most of them need soaking for at least eight hours before cooking. All dried pulses should be boiled rapidly for at least ten minutes during cooking to remove toxins (poisons).

If you use dried beans and pulses in a meal allow 50 grams dry weight per person. If you are using canned beans allow 200 grams per person.

Tofu

Tofu is made from soya bean curd. Firm tofu can be sliced and cubed and used in stir fries and stews. Soft, silken tofu is made into dips and sauces.

Textured vegetable protein

Textured vegetable protein (TVP) is made from soya bean flour which has been processed and made into minced or chunk form.
When used in its dry form it will swell to three or four times its dry weight. You only need about 25 grams per person and it can be made into burgers, shepherd's pie, curries and stews.

Sainsbury's Mexican chilli style soya mince

Quorn

Quorn is the **brand name** for a food product made from a plant called myco-protein which occurs naturally in soil. Through a process called fermentation the product can be made on a large scale. Under the microscope myco-protein looks like meat fibres so Quorn has been marketed as an alternative to meat. Quorn is sold in pieces, minced and in dishes such as burgers, sausages and ready meals.

For development work using Quorn see pages 46–50 in the Teacher's Resource Pack.

Arrum

At last, a 'healthy' meat

A chicken substitute made from extruded pea protein has been developed for the health-conscious wanting to cut down on fat. Lucas Industries, part of the food group Dalgety, claims the meat substitute **Arrum** is the best match for the texture of chicken, better than soya or Quorn. Arrum is high in protein and contains the same level of fibre as a jacket potato. Meat, on the other hand, contains no fibre. In chicken, 32 per cent of the calories come from fat. Arrum has just 11 per cent of calories from fat, all of it the healthy unsaturated variety. So far it is available only in the cottage pie in Birds Eye's new Meatfree range, at £1.39.

Daily Mail, *22 November 1996*

Foods from animals	Vegetarian alternatives
meat, fish, chicken	TVP, Quorn, tofu, beans, lentils, nuts, seeds, cereals
milk and its products (yogurt, ice-cream)	soya milk and products made from it – e.g. frozen tofu dessert
cheese	vegetarian cheese made from non-animal rennet
animal fats such as lard, animal suet, dripping	margarines which are not made from fats, vegetarian lards and suet
stock cubes made from meat, chicken and fish	vegetarian stock cubes and products such as Marmite
gelatine and jellies	products that are thickened with starch or agar-agar, not gelatine

How you can make vegetarian choices instead of animal food choices

Adapting a recipe for a vegetarian

Quite often you will see traditional recipes for food products that are adapted to suit vegetarians.

Cottage pie recipe	Vegetarian choices
100 g minced beef	Replace by using Quorn, TVP, tofu, lentils or selection of beans.
30 g chopped bacon	Remove – you may need to add a little salt or spices and herbs to the recipe.
half an onion	half an onion
1 tbs tomato paste	1tbs tomato paste
1 large potato	1 large potato
50 g grated cheese	Make sure the cheese is suitable for vegetarians.

Adapting a cottage pie recipe for a vegetarian

For example, lasagne can be made using Quorn, sweet and sour dishes use tofu, and burgers and sausages can be made from beans and lentils.

Left is a recipe for Cottage pie which shows how the ingredients can be adapted to suit vegetarians. The traditional Cottage pie is a layer of minced beef with a topping of mashed potato and grated cheese.

Questions

1 What food products are used by some vegetarians as meat replacements? Give examples of food products using these ingredients.

2 Describe the food product Arrum discussed in the newspaper article. What is it made from and what are the claims made for this product? How do you think Arrum will be used in food products?

Design a soup (1)

Your brief is to design a soup which could be sold either in the winter or summer months. Use the information on the following pages to give you design ideas. You need to work out:

- the ingredients you will use for the soup and the uses of those ingredients in the soup
- a detailed specification for the soup
- the process used to make the soup
- how the soup will be packaged for sale.

Soup facts for design ideas

Chilled fresh soups were first sold in Britain in the 1980s. Research shows that people like soup which tastes as if it is home-made and is made from natural ingredients, with few E numbers.

- Ready-to-eat soups are sold canned, dried and fresh (chilled).
- Most of the sales (66 per cent) occur between October and April.
- If people are 'grazing and snacking' – which means eating small amounts of food throughout the day – a soup is like a small meal.
- Soups with recognizable names such as 'Tomato soup', sell the best.
- Soup can be nutritious, providing carbohydrates, protein, dietary fibre, vitamins and minerals.

Case study

New Covent Garden Soup Company

In 1988 the New Covent Garden Soup Company launched its range of fresh soups in the UK. The company chooses recipe ideas with seasonal vegetables and uses traditional domestic cooking methods which are adapted for large-scale production. They produce over 7 million litres of soup a year and are constantly developing new recipe ideas. This company has more than half of the chilled soup market.

The company produces a range of recipes which are available all year round, separate Winter and Summer ranges and a Soup of the month.

STANDARD RANGE
(all year round)

Carrot and Coriander 'V'
Vichyssoise (Leek and Potato) 'V'
Cream of Chicken with Lemon and Tarragon
Mushroom with Parsley and Garlic 'V'
Spinach with Nutmeg 'V'
Tuscan Bean 'V'
Soup of the month
Minestrone 'V'
Asparagus 'V'
Lentil and Tomato with Cumin and Coriander 'V'

The standard range of New Covent Garden soups

How are soup recipes developed?

The recipes for New Covent Garden soups come from a variety of sources. The New Product Development team may create new recipes or develop existing ones, or ask other people to design new recipes.

The recipe opposite for Mushroom soup with parsley and garlic was created by Caroline Jeremy when she worked as a freelance recipe developer for the company. She designed a small-scale recipe in the kitchen of her flat and, with the help of technologists, increased the proportions of the recipe for large scale production.

Mushroom Soup
with Parsley and Garlic

This is one of the first recipes ever created by Caroline Jeremy, now our Marketing Director, in the kitchen of her own flat when she was working as a freelance recipe developer for the soup company back at the very beginning of 1987. The recipe uses vegetable stock after the company received many letters from vegetarian soup lovers who felt excluded.

Preparation and cooking time: 40 minutes
Serves: 6

> 25 g butter
> ½ medium onion, finely chopped
> 1 garlic clove, finely chopped
> 40 g plain flour
> 700 ml vegetable stock (use water and a vegetable stock cube)
> 250 g mushrooms, sliced
> 1 tbs finely chopped fresh flat-leaf parsley
> 75 ml single cream
> salt and freshly ground black pepper

To garnish:

2 tbs finely chopped fresh flat-leaf parsley

Melt half the butter and cook the onion and garlic gently for 5 minutes in a covered saucepan, without colouring. Stir in the flour and cook gently for one minute, stirring. Gradually add the stock, stirring all the time. Add half the mushrooms and the parsley. Cover, bring to the boil and simmer gently for about 10–15 minutes until the vegetables are tender. Cool a little, then purée in a liquidizer.

In the remaining butter, sauté the rest of the mushrooms for 5 minutes until they begin to brown, then add to the puréed soup. Simmer gently for 3 minutes. Stir in the cream and taste for seasoning. Serve garnished with chopped parsley.

The New Covent Garden Company's 'Book of Soups'

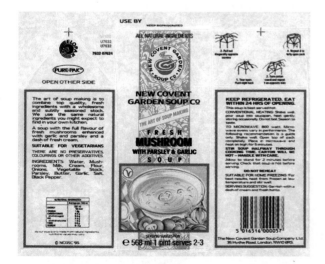

Mushroom soup with Parsley and Garlic

Questions

Use the recipe above for the mushroom soup to answer the questions.

1 How many people does this soup serve? Work out the weight of a portion of this soup – add up the weight of all the ingredients and divide by six. (**Note:** To keep things simple, let the measurement in ml be the same as grams, so 250 ml = 250 grams.)

2 List the ingredients in the soup in the order they would appear on a food label – the heaviest ingredient is listed first.

3 Why would a food company choose to make some of its products, such as soups, suitable for vegetarians?

Design a soup (2)

How is soup made on a large scale?

The New Convent Garden Soup Company started making its soups on a large scale in the late 1980s. At the time there was plenty of ready-made soup sold in cans or dried and packaged. This company decided to sell fresh soups with a home-made flavour, which were made from high-quality ingredients that were natural, and with no additives.

The company packs its soups in colourful cartons which can be used in the microwave oven. It started with three soup products – Chicken soup with Lemon and Tarragon, Carrot and Coriander, and Vichyssoise – a soup made from leeks and potatoes.

Today the company has a large range of soups, including the ever-changing 'soup of the month' range.

Special points

Chicken soups are made at the end of the day to avoid mixing the product with vegetarian foods. The company makes about 35,000 cartons of soup each day.

Making soup on a large scale

1 Fresh ingredients arrive at the factory each day. The vegetables are cleaned, peeled and chopped to the sizes required ready for cooking.

2 Ingredients are weighed according to computer instructions.

3 The soup is cooked in giant saucepans under pressure.

4 Computers control the time, temperature and amount of water added – the time varies according to the ingredients used.

5 An agitator mixes the ingredients to make a smooth soup.

6 Cartons are filled with hot soup, then sealed and passed through a metal detector.

7 The cartons are chilled to a very low temperature in a cold water tunnel and packed for despatch.

8 Quality assurance procedures are carried out throughout production.

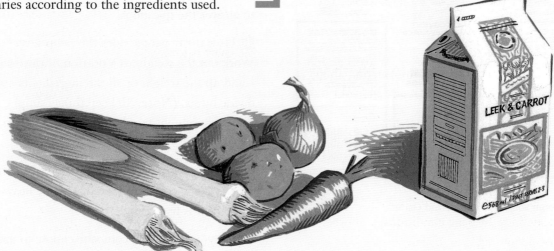

Fresh vegetables are processed into soup and cartons filled

Product description

When a company has decided upon the type of soup it wants to make, it needs a clear description of the product. The description could be listed under the headings 'Appearance', 'Mouthfeel' and 'Flavour'. This description is kept as a reference. When the soup is made, the final product can be checked to see if it meets this description.

Specification for Winter tomato soup

This specification shows the details that a company might use to describe a soup for manufacture.

Product description	Winter tomato soup
appearance	a terracotta red, with pieces of chickpeas, tomato seed, oregano and parsley
mouthfeel	between single and double cream in thickness, seeds and chickpeas help texture
flavour	fresh tomato and oregano with peppery aftertaste

Specification for tomato soup

Source: The New Covent Garden Soup Company

Other information

The company needs a lot of information about the product before it can be made and sold.

- The suppliers of the ingredients have to make sure that they meet the specification and quality standards.
- The product must be safe to eat.
- The label is designed and the pack must show the shelf life, storage conditions, and other information required by law.
- The company has to be sure that the product can be transported safely and efficiently for sale.

Uses of ingredients in soup

Each of the ingredients in the soup has one or more functions in the recipe.

Uses of ingredients	Ingredients used
flavour	butter, onion, mushrooms, parsley, garlic, salt and pepper
colour	mushrooms, parsley
texture	mushrooms
thickening	flour, cream
thinning	vegetable stock

A bowl of soup and the functions of the ingredients

Pages 17–20 in the Teacher's Resource Pack has further work.

To do

1 Choose some soup recipes from a book and, for each soup, make a list of the uses of each of the ingredients using the headings on the chart below.

Uses of ingredients	Ingredients used
flavour	
colour	
texture	
thickening	
thinning	

2 Write a specification for one of the following soups, using the headings 'Appearance', 'Mouthfeel' and 'Flavour'.

Soups: chunky beef and vegetable soup, cheesy vegetable soup, fish soup

Design and make a sponge pudding (1)

Your brief is to design a range of sponge puddings with different flavours and colours.

The process

1 Choose ingredients for the **basic recipe.**
2 Add flavour, texture and toppings.
3 Choose a mixing method.
4 Choose a cooking method.
5 Draw up a specification.
6 Decide how the food should be packaged.
7 Make and test the product.
8 Evaluate the results.

1 Basic recipe ingredients

Many recipes for cakes, biscuits and breads use basic recipes as the starting point for design. Basic recipes have been tried and tested over the years and produce successful results. You can design around these basic recipes by adding other ingredients to give flavour, colour and texture.

For this brief, adapt a basic sponge recipe which is based upon the following proportions:

The weight of one egg: same weight of caster sugar, soft margarine and white self raising flour. So a basic recipe could be:

60 g caster sugar, 60 g soft margarine, 1 size 3 egg, 60 g self raising flour.

This recipe makes four small individual puddings.

Basic ingredients for a cake

Uses of ingredients in a cake

The basic ingredients for a sponge cake are flour, sugar, fat and egg and have the following uses:

bulking, sweetening, helps form structure, raising agent, holds air, flavour.

Choosing the basic ingredients

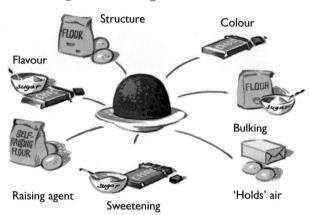

Flavour · Structure · Colour · Bulking · Raising agent · Sweetening · 'Holds' air

Function of ingredients in a chocolate cake

Adapt your recipe and choose the type of ingredients you would like to use. For example, flour: wholemeal self-raising; sugar: caster sugar; fats: soft margarine.

Basic sponge cake ingredients			
flours	sugars	fats	egg
white self-raising flour	caster sugar	soft margarine	size 3
wholemeal self-raising	granulated sugar	hard margarine	
stoneground self-raising	icing sugar	butter	
plain flour plus baking powder			

Chart to show types of ingredients for a cake

84

2 Flavour, texture and toppings

Flavour ideas – vanilla essence, chocolate, coffee, lemon juice

Texture ideas – chocolate chips, dried fruits, seeds such as sesame seeds

Toppings – chopped apple, dates, pineapple, lemon curd, golden syrup

Heinz Chocolate sponge pudding

Ingredients for flavour and texture

3 Mixing method

Mix the sponge by the following methods.

- All-in-one method – put all the ingredients in a bowl and beat with an electric mixer.
- Traditional method – beat the fat (margarine or butter) and sugar, add the egg and stir in the flour.

4 Cooking method

Cook the sponge in one of three different ways.

- Steam it over a saucepan of boiling water.
- Bake it in the oven.
- Cook it in a microwavable dish in the microwave oven.

5 Specifications

You need to include:

- the ingredients for each product in the range
- the methods for making and cooking the product
- the size, shape and description of product
- what you want the product to look like and taste like
- the packaging that could be used.

6 Packaging

Will you choose to sell it chilled as a ready meal or canned such as the Heinz Chocolate sponge pudding? You could decide to produce the sponge as a dried cake mix in a packet.

Questions

1 If the basic recipe shown in this section makes four sponge puddings, list the quantities of ingredients needed to make:

a 12 puddings   **b** 20 puddings.

2 Write a report on your results and suggest why your product could be successful. Then answer these questions.

Who might buy your products? Who would eat them? At what time of day might they be eaten? Would they be served as part of a meal, or on their own?

Give your reasons.

Design and make a sponge pudding (2)

Large-scale production

When sponge puddings are made on a large scale in a factory, the company has a clear specification for the ingredients, the size, shape and description of the results, the packaging and the process of manufacture.

Specification

Ingredients

Cake flour, raising agent designed to specification, margarine blended for taste and ability to hold air, sugar (size of granules is specified in mm), egg is pasteurized and can be dried to avoid problems with salmonella (food poisoning bacteria).

Size, shape and description

This may say 'dome shaped, light, pale coloured sponge with fruit topping'.

Packaging

For example, served in microwavable, plastic pots with plastic top and cardboard outer case.

Process

Ingredients weighed by computer, mixed in large scale mixer, cooked in an oven, cooled, packed and stored for distribution.

A sponge pudding

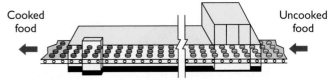

A travelling oven – baked goods pass through the oven

Industrial cooking

Large-scale bakers can use a travelling oven to bake sponge puddings. It is called a travelling oven because the sponges pass along inside the oven (travel through) on a conveyor belt. A conveyor belt is a long belt which carries products through a system such as baking the sponges. The raw sponge is baked first at a high temperature to help the raising agent push up the dough, and then at a lower temperature to cook the pudding and prevent burning.

Making products the same

Why do food products have to be the same size and shape? If you were buying some sponge cakes from a bakery, you would expect the sponge cakes to be similar in size, shape and colour. It would be unfair for the bakery to sell large and small sponge cakes for the same price and customers would become unhappy!

When you are designing a food product, think about how you would make it the same every time. When products are made on a large scale, they must be the same size, shape, colour and texture. Quality checks throughout the process make sure the product meets these standards. You will need to set up quality checks throughout the making process.

Tolerance levels

The **tolerance level** is the amount of flexibility allowed in a recipe so that the product meets the standards set down in the specification. For example, the specification for the sponge puddings may state that the puddings should weigh 50 grams each, with a tolerance level of 5 grams more or less on that weight. So the puddings could weigh 55 grams or 45 grams and still meet the standards.

When you are designing the sponge puddings and have written your specification, decide which aspects of the specification need some level of tolerance.

Colour tolerance

You could choose to specify the colour of the cooked sponge pudding. You can use a colour chart from a paint manufacturer to choose and show the colour match for the cooked sponge. Choose other colours close to this colour match that you would also accept for the finished sponge. This is the tolerance level for colour for the sponge. When the sponge is cooked, compare your result with the colour chart and see how nearly it matches your colour specification. If it is too dark or too pale, suggest what changes you may need to make to the process.

Weight, size and shape

The puddings should all be made to roughly the same size and shape. Suggest how much the puddings should weigh, and draw the design and label it to show the expected size and shape. Indicate the tolerance levels for the weight, size and shape. How much more or how much less could it weigh, how much bigger or how much smaller could it be in size and shape against the original specification? When the puddings are cooked, check the weight, size and shape against these details and see which of the puddings fits within the tolerance levels. If changes are needed to the process to make the puddings fit the standards, suggest how these changes could be made.

Ocean pearl	W1		Peach sorbet	A1
Creamy peach	W2		Burnt orange	A2
Oyster	W3		Cayenne	A3
Peach melba	W4		Paprika blush	A4
Vanilla	W5		Chilli	A5
Mellow mist	W6		Rosewood	A6
Tender dawn	W7		Copper kiln	A7
Mushroom mood	W8		Firenze	A8
Honeycomb	W9			
Harvest dawn	W10			
Californian tan	W11			
Jamaican flush	W12			

Colour charts from paint shops can be used to match the colour of food products

Questions

1 If food products are for sale, why do they have to be the same size and shape? Give *three* reasons for your answer.

2 What is meant by 'tolerance level'? Give an example of how you could use tolerance levels when designing a food product.

3 List four other basic recipes which you could adapt for product design.

Ready-to-eat meals and desserts (1)

Your brief is to design and make a ready-to-eat meal or dessert which could be sold in a supermarket chill cabinet.

The process

1 Research the ranges of ready-to-eat chilled meals and desserts to get ideas.
2 Decide on the range of meals or desserts to trial.
3 Test out ideas, and taste the results.
4 Draw up a specification.
5 Make and test the product.
6 Evaluate the results.
7 Decide how the meal or dessert will be processed and packaged.
8 If the product is to be reheated, write the instructions.

Research

We eat more and more ready-to-eat meals and desserts. This chart shows how these products can be processed for sale. The range of food products includes canned, frozen, dried, **long-life** and chilled meals and desserts. When you design a ready-to-eat meal, think about how it could be processed and packaged before it is ready for sale. By investigating the range of processed meals for sale, you will get ideas for developing design ideas for a chilled meal or dessert.

Chilled turkey dinner
Frozen ready meal
Chilled sausage hot pot
Frozen fish and chip meal
Canned meal
Dessert in a carton
Canned snack meal
Canned sponge pudding
Chilled vegetal sweet and sou

Ready-to-eat meals

For more information on the processing of ready meals see page 51 in the Teacher's Resource Pack.

	Canned meal	Frozen meal	Dried meal	Long-life meal	Chilled meal
What is it?	A ready cooked meal in a can.	A prepared cooked frozen meal.	Dried food in a packet.	A ready cooked, sealed meal.	A ready prepared, refrigerated meal.
Where is it kept?	On open shelves (ambient storage).	In freezer compartments at –18°C.	On open shelves (ambient storage).	On open shelves (ambient storage).	In refrigerators at 5°C.
How long will it keep?	1–5 years depending on the food type.	1–12 months depending on the food type.	Up to 24 months depending on the food type.	Up to 15 months after date of manufacture.	1–3 days depending on the food type.
Comments	Easy to store and safe from harmful bacteria. Heating only is needed.	Freezing does not destroy bacteria, so food must be thoroughly cooked.	Food needs to reabsorb water and then be thoroughly heated.	Easy to store and since they are already cooked, they just need reheating.	The food must be thoroughly heated right through to 70°C for 2 minutes.

How ready-to-eat food products can be processed for sale

Chilled meals

Chilled meals may be stored in the chill cabinet in a supermarket. Popular chilled meals include shepherd's pie, curries, Chinese sweet and sour dishes, chilli con carne, fisherman's pie, lasagne, rice and prawns.

Ready-to-eat chilled desserts

Ready-to-eat chilled desserts can be processed and packaged in similar ways to ready-to-eat meals. Types of ready-to-eat desserts which may be sold from the chill cabinet include yogurts, trifles, chocolate mousse, cheesecakes with a variety of toppings such as strawberry, raspberry or blackcurrant, filled meringues, baked sponge puddings and bread and butter pudding. Some of these desserts can be eaten cold, and others need reheating for serving.

To do

Research the range of meals and desserts that are available in the chill cabinet of supermarkets. Record details of the cost of the products, the weight and number of servings for each product. Compare the results of your research with those of others.

Cook-chill foods

Cook-chill foods are fully cooked, fast chilled and then stored at low temperatures above freezing point (0–3°C). They can be kept for up to five days, which include the day of cooking and the day of eating. The food must not be eaten after this time as the quality and safety decreases.

Questions

1 What are the different ways of preparing and packing ready-to-eat meals?

2 What temperature controls are essential during the production of cook-chill food products? Why are these controls necessary?

Cook-chill foods	Control checks
Choose good quality foods	Store the perishable raw foods at temperatures around 5°C.
Prepare food quickly and cook thoroughly	Keep food out of the danger zone 5°C to 63°C and cook thoroughly so that the centre of the food reaches 70°C for 2 minutes.
Chill the food quickly	Food should be chilled as soon as it is cooked. Chill to between 0°C and 3°C within 90 minutes.
Store the food product	Store at temperatures between 0°C and 3°C.
Distribution and storage	The food should be kept at or below 3°C until reheating.
Time for storage	This should not exceed 5 days including the day of cooking and eating.
Reheating	Reheat food when you are ready to eat it – no longer than 30 minutes after it is removed from chill. Heat so that the centre of the food reaches 70°C for 2 minutes.
Serving	Serve as soon as possible and do not allow the temperature of the food to drop below 63°C.

Chart to show cook-chill process

Ready-to-eat meals and desserts (2)

Careful temperature and time controls and good, hygienic working practices are essential throughout the process of making a cook-chill product.

As you make the product, make sure that you control the temperature throughout the process to follow the guidelines shown below.

Reheating in the microwave

If the product is to be reheated, you need to write the reheating instructions from cold.

Investigation to find out how long food takes to reheat in a microwave cooker

You need

- microwave cooker, temperature probe, stopwatch, bacterial wipes for the food probe
- the food product to be reheated in a microwave container

Method

1   Place the food product in the microwave container for reheating.

2   Draw up a chart to show the time in consecutive 15-second intervals, with a column for recording the temperature. You can use a chart like this.

Cooking time	Temperature at centre	Temperature at edge
start		
15 seconds		
30 seconds		
45 seconds		

3   After each period of 15 seconds, take the temperature at the centre and edge of the food. Insert the temperature probe to a depth of 2 cm and record the results when the reading has settled. Rinse the probe in water and then clean it with an anti bacterial wipe after each insertion. The anti bacterial wipe kills bacteria and reduces the likelihood of cross-contamination of bacteria from one part of the food to another.

4   Record how long it takes for the centre of the food to reach 70°C for two minutes. This is the reheating time for your product using the specific microwave cooker that you have used for this experiment. Other microwave cookers will vary in their cooking time depending on the wattage of each cooker.

Note: You can carry out a similar investigation to find out how long the product will take to reach 70°C for two minutes in a conventional or fan oven. The reheating time will take longer by this method, so set the cooking time intervals on the chart at five-minute intervals instead of fifteen second intervals.

Questions

Explain how you would use a temperature probe to measure the temperature of a food product. Why is it important to clean the probe with an anti-bacterial wipe after insertion into food?

Food design and the Law

When food producers are designing food products, there are several important Acts and Regulations that they must follow.

The Food Labelling Regulations 1995

The Food Labelling Regulations 1995 apply to all food for human consumption, with the exception of natural mineral waters. By law a food label must contain the information below:

- the name of the product
- ingredients in descending order of weight
- the net weight of the product
- name and address of manufacturer
- place of origin of the food
- instructions for use if these are needed
- the 'use by' or 'best before' date to identify the shelf life
- any special storage or use conditions.

This information must appear on the packaging, on a label attached to, or clearly visible through, the packaging. (There are some exceptions.)

The Food Safety (General Food Hygiene) Regulations 1995

These regulations lay down standards for premises and equipment, personal hygiene and other measures to ensure the safety and wholesomeness of food. Requirements included in the regulations are hazard analysis and food hygiene training. The regulations cover the preparation, processing, manufacturing, packaging, storing, transportation, distribution, handling and selling of food products.

The Food Safety (Temperature Control) Regulations 1995

The regulations require foods which are likely to support the growth of pathogenic micro-organisms or the formation of toxins to be held at or below 8°C. Cooked or reheated food that needs to be kept hot must be kept at a temperature at or above 63°C by food businesses.

The Food Safety Act 1990

This Act is designed to help reduce the number of food-borne illness such as food poisoning and contamination. It is an offence to sell, offer or have in possession for sale any food which is harmful to health, contaminated, falsely labelled, advertised or presented, or not of the nature, substance or quality demanded by the purchaser. Failure to meet these requirements can result in fines and/or imprisonment.

The Sale and Supply of Goods Act 1994

The Sale and Supply of Goods Act 1994 states that goods must be of satisfactory quality, fit for their purpose and as described.

The Sale of Goods Act 1979

The Sale of Goods Act 1979 protects consumers when they buy goods. Goods must be of a 'satisfactory quality' and the Act gives a list of quality to be taken into account.

The Trade Descriptions Act 1968

It is an offence to make false or misleading statements about goods or mislead about services, accommodation or facilities.

The Weights and Measures Act 1985

This Act states that the quantity of the contents must be marked on the packaging by weight, volume or number. The Act makes it an offence to give short weight or inadequate quantity, or to mark goods with the wrong amount.

Questions

Which Act or Regulation helps protect us if:

a food is not properly labelled
b food is not stored at the correct temperature
c goods are not of a satisfactory quality
d the goods are the wrong weight?

Using IT

You can use information technology in many ways to help with food technology work. Here are some ideas.

Word processing and desktop publishing

- Smarten up your work by using computer printouts.
- Create ideas for recipes and menus using different fonts and letter sizes.
- Use clip-art, computer graphics and drawing packages to enhance work.
- Draw charts for HACCP and flow diagrams.

Graphics packages

These can be used for:

- sketching and modifying design ideas and working on colourways
- creating **logos** and simple packet designs
- drawing packaging nets with food labels and logos.

Spreadsheets

These can be used to carry out or prepare:

- nutritional analysis
- costing of foods
- tasting charts – rating, ranking and star diagrams
- attribute analysis
- temperature control and monitoring
- price check on foods – comparative shopping
- calculation of quantities for batch production.

Databases

These can be used to store and retrieve:

- nutritional analysis information
- food ingredient prices
- lists of food additives and their function
- recipes
- questionnaires.

Sensors and control

Use for monitoring temperature changes.

Using a video and digital camera

Import images into documents – take photos of food designs, research information and experimental work.

Scanners

- Scan in images to use in project work, and generate ideas.
- Scan in cross sections of food products.

CD ROMS and Internet

These provide up-to-date information sources.

Modelling using a computer

You can:

- model the nutritional profile of a food product
- test out new recipe formulations with costings.

Information Technology available

Nutrients, produced by Hampshire Microtechnology Centre, is a computer program that can analyse the nutritional value of foods and produce nutritional labels for food products. Facilities in the program include:

- a database of over 800 foods
- printouts of the analysis of food nutrients
- graphical displays of information
- portion sizes, nutritional labels.

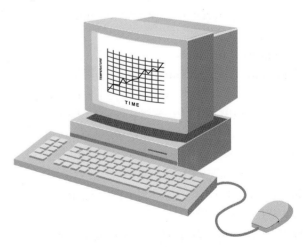

Graph showing temperature changes in food

This printout shows the way *Nutrients* is used to create a pizza label which contains nutrition information and artwork for the product, as well as a list of ingredients and other labelling information.

PIZZA
Bacon and Tomato

Label from food list   Pizza
Total cooked weight   580 g
Number of portions   3

Nutrition information – Pizza		
	Typical values	
	per 100 g	**per serving**
Energy	1287 kJ	2487 kJ
	307 kcal	594 kcal
Protein	9.68 g	18.7 g
Carbohydrate	22.6 g	43.6 g
Fat	20.5 g	39.6 g

A printout of a pizza label from *Nutrients*

Using Information Technology in the food industry

Here are some of the ways that information technology is used in the food industry.

- Images and design ideas – communicated to customers using a phone line.
- Market research surveys and results.
- Process management in the factory.
- Modelling bacterial growth to determine food safety.
- Costing food products.
- Temperature control and monitoring changes.
- Distribution management – keeping records of where food products are being sent and stored.
- Stock control – shops monitor the amount of goods in stock and order more when needed.
- Nutritional analysis of food products.
- Bar codes – these help with stock control and ordering.
- Artwork designs and packaging designs can be transmitted around the world.

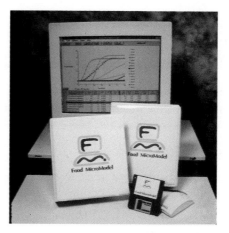

Modelling bacterial growth to determine food safety

Food MicroModel is a computer program which is used to predict bacterial growth in food products. The formulation of the food product is analysed by the program, and predictions made about the growth of certain bacteria over a period of time, under different storage conditions.

Uses of computers in industry

To do

1 Find out about the range of information technology facilities that are available in your school. Suggest ways that each program or piece of equipment could be used for food technology work.

2 Describe ways you could use the Internet to find information for your food technology research.

Glossary

additives substances added to foods in small amounts to perform a function such as to preserve, colour or flavour a product.

aroma the smell of a product.

Arrum a chicken substitute made from extruded pea protein, high in protein and fibre.

basic recipe a recipe which has been tested to show that it works – used for cakes, bread, scones, pastry.

biodegradable materials materials that break down if they are left in the soil – for example, cardboard packaging.

blind tasting to taste something without seeing it.

brand name a product name with a logo such as Heinz baked beans.

canning preserving food in a tin can by heating and sealing under vacuum.

concept screening a way of deciding which products should be chosen for development.

cook-chill food which has been cooked, fast chilled and then stored at low temperatures.

critical control point a step in the process of making a product that must be controlled to avoid the risk of food poisoning.

cross-contamination the transfer of a substance from one area to another such as bacteria.

danger zone the temperature range in which bacteria thrive (5°C to 63°C).

database a set of data held on a computer – for example, nutrition information.

date-mark shows the shelf life of the product.

disassemble to take a product apart to get design information.

e the big e beside the weight of a product means that the average quantity must be accurate.

E numbers the number given to an additive to show that it has been approved by the EC.

ethnic foods food products from countries other than Britain.

EU European Union.

feedback used by control systems to see if the output is correct.

flavour mixture of taste and smell.

food hygiene keeping food clean.

food probe used to measure the temperature of food.

food technology the process of converting raw materials into edible food products including meals.

formulation the recipe for the product with the exact amount of ingredients required.

HACCP hazard analysis and critical control point.

hazard anything that can cause harm to the consumer.

high-risk foods high protein foods which encourage bacterial growth.

image board a display of pictures and drawings to give ideas about a range of products.

imperial measures the old system of measuring food in ounces, pounds and pints.

IT information technology – using computers.

key words important words which may relate to the design brief.

logo the symbol of a company used on products.

long-life a product is able to be kept for a long time due to heat processing and the method of packaging.

MAP modified atmosphere packaging.

metric measures measuring in grams, kilos, litres and millilitres.

modelling to experiment with an idea without actually carrying it out – you can model the nutritional value of a food product.

piping hot food food that is heated to 70°C for 2 minutes.

portion a portion for one is the amount of food that satisfies the needs of one person.

primary processing the first stage of a food before is made into something else.

purée to blend to a smooth mixture.

quality assurance a system that is set up before a product is made which lays down procedures for making a quality, safe product.

quality control steps in the process of making a product to make sure that it meets the standards. Faulty products are removed.

Quorn myco-protein which can be used as a meat substitute.

raw materials the basic ingredients that are made into food products. For example, apples are the raw materials used for apple pies.

recycled packaging such as glass, metal and paper that is reused or made into other products.

salmonella bacteria which cause food poisoning.

secondary processing foods which are made from others – milk made into cheese.

sensory descriptors words which describe taste, smell, texture and flavour.

sensory properties of food properties related to taste, smell, texture and flavour.

shelf life how long a food product can be kept, making sure it is safe to eat and good quality.

simulation an activity which models a process to see if it works properly.

system made up of input, process, output and feedback.

tofu soya bean curd, which can be used in stir fried meals and stews.

tolerance level the amount of flexibility allowed when making a product in terms of weight, colour, size, so that it meets quality standards.

TVP textured vegetable protein made from soya bean flour and used to substitute meat.

vegan a vegetarian who does not eat any kind of food made from animals.

vegetarian a vegetarian eats no meat, poultry or fish and avoids products made from slaughtered animals.

Index

Answers from questions on Portion Control (page 62)

a 165 g, b 25–30 g, c 60 g, d 420 g, e 410 g, f 50 g

MAFF – Food Portion Sizes Second Editio